Beat the
Emotional Games
That Sabotage
Your Finances

MONEY
TROUBLE

Thomas C. Manheim

Adams Media
Avon, Massachusetts

Published by
Adams Media, an F+W Publications Company
57 Littlefield Street, Avon, MA 02322 U.S.A.
www.adamsmedia.com

ISBN: 1-59337-095-4

Printed in Canada.

J I H G F E D C B A

Library of Congress Cataloging-in-Publication Data
Manheim, Thomas C.
Money trouble / Thomas C. Manheim.
        p.   cm.
ISBN 1-59337-095-4
1. Finance, Personal--Psychological aspects.
2. Money--Psychological aspects. I. Title.
        HG179.M2635   2005
    332.024--dc22   2004010017

This publication is designed to provide accurate and authoritative information with
regard to the subject matter covered. It is sold with the understanding that the
publisher is not engaged in rendering legal, accounting, or other professional
advice. If legal advice or other expert assistance is required, the services of a
competent professional person should be sought.
    —From a *Declaration of Principles* jointly adopted by a Committee of the
American Bar Association and a Committee of Publishers and Associations

Many of the designations used by manufacturers and sellers to distinguish their
products are claimed as trademarks. Where those designations appear in this
book and Adams Media was aware of a trademark claim, the designations have
been printed in initial capital letters.

Interior illustration © 2000 Artville, LLC.

To all of humanity
In search of greater clarity
and purpose with money

Contents

Preface

My life changed abruptly at 3:30 P.M. on Saturday, January 9, 1999.

My son Derek and I were biking to baseball practice when a car ran a red light, hitting Derek and throwing him fifteen feet into the air. As I attended to his bleeding, abraded body on the pavement, I had an epiphany. At some level inside, I knew that when Derek healed (and, miraculously, he did), I would not—could not—go back to burying myself in my routine. Life was too fleeting, too fragile for that.

Instead, I vowed to get in touch with my life's purpose and to pursue it, no matter what. Thus, I later went to Nepal and lived in a monastery for ten days, pondering the accident and the future. What I decided was that I had to thrust myself outside my comfort zone and do something startlingly different. I didn't want to look back twenty-five or thirty years later and wonder how my life would have turned out if only I had followed my passion and used whatever skill and knowledge I had to be of service to others.

So, I left a successful eighteen-year career as a stockbroker. (Most recently, I'd been Senior Vice President/Investments at Paine Webber, where I'd won numerous awards and managed more than $175 million in assets.) And I founded The Love of Money, Inc., a financial counseling firm that helps individuals, couples, and organizations integrate life goals and spiritual values into their relationship with money.

I began to look more deeply into how I and others use—or are used by—money. What I found out is that in one way or another, we all learned—or are still learning—to play the game of money. As is true with personal relationships, we each bring a particular role and set of rules to that interaction.

Think of these games as psychological transactions between ourselves and money, and between ourselves and others about money. The games are based partly on conscious choices and solid experience and partly on unconscious needs, desires, and beliefs—"shoulds," "coulds," and "musts." How well we understand these games and our role in them often determines how satisfied we are with the outcomes.

This book aims to help. It presents fifteen core Money Games that we play to get, keep, use, or deplete money in order to get our needs met. Each game is presented with the common rules, roles, beliefs, and secrets that anchor the game for us. By consciously exploring these games, we can learn about the emotional triggers that set off our own games. We can understand the belief systems that form their foundation. And we can then either continue to play the games, manage them better, or choose to replace them with more conscious actions.

To preserve client confidentiality, I have altered the identities of all persons cited in case studies. Further, in some cases, I have combined more than one actual person to create a composite character.

In the following pages, you'll have the chance to explore your acquired money belief systems and decide if you want to keep them or jettison them. You'll be able to craft a plan for your money future and shape how you proceed with money. You'll heighten your money awareness and learn how to be a more conscious player.

Above all, you'll be able to choose to gain some control over your financial life. You'll be able to make conscious decisions and circumvent unwise outcomes. And you'll be able to put more balanced money practices to work for you.

Let the games begin!

Acknowledgments

This book is the product of many hands. I'd particularly like to give thanks to Dr. Uta Hoehne, my mentor and coach, whose belief in this project inspired me. To Dale Fetherling, who was instrumental in designing my book proposal, guiding me through the publishing world, and editing this book to be more reader-friendly. To Pamela Adams, who assisted me in organizing the material while diligently editing and sharing her knowledge of the publishing industry. To Frank Weimann, my agent, who quickly found a buyer for my book. To Jill Alexander at Adams Media, the book's publisher, who was a delight to work with.

I would also like to give thanks to my family members, who have respected the creative process and kept me in balance throughout this lengthy journey: in particular to my son Derek, who shared his spiritual insights the day of his accident; Dana, my daughter, whose fun-loving nature brings me back to reality; especially my wife, Lynn, who has been unwavering and supportive with her love throughout the birthing process of this book; and to my mother, Paula, who has been by my side offering her love and kudos along the way.

More thanks to our friends Liz and George Stimson, who have cheered and encouraged me, and to my friends in the brokerage community, Andy Grant, Tom Schroeder, and Betsy Delong. To fellow therapists Claire Chateauneuf, a terrific comrade and colleague; Woody Fulmor, a gifted Rolfer and friend; as well as to Maureen Moss and Lynn Dries-Daffner. To family friends Gold, Theis, Anennlo, and Vetter. And to my brother and sister and in-laws' families: Bill Manheim, Jaimie Sennett, Bob and Nancy Powell, and Mark Powell.

Finally, to the following groups that also helped: the monthly book club members Mark, Llizane, Cheryl, Maura, and Kisha; the families associated with the Del Mar Sharks soccer teams, whom my children have played for and who took my surveys; Solana Beach North Coast Toastmasters, who listened to my various presentations on money; and the California Association of Marriage Family Therapists.

Tom Manheim
Del Mar, California

Introduction

Are You Conscious or
Unconscious about Money?

Money. We love it. We hate it. We are thrilled when we have it, and we worry when we don't. Often we want it more than anything. We use money to do good things for others and good things for ourselves. But sometimes we misuse others because of money. And sometimes we misuse ourselves to get it.

Money pervades our lives in both conscious and unconscious ways. That is, we see it very consciously when we get a paycheck. We feel it and smell it when we go to an ATM and pull out a handful of twenties. Or we watch it hawk-eyed, peering at the teller's hands while he or she doles out cash. We fold it into our wallets and wonder how it disappears so quickly into the gas tank, the mortgage, the kids' tuition, the roulette wheel, or the charity bazaar. By the weekend or month's end, or by tax time, we puzzle over where it went. That's conscious. Painful, perhaps, but conscious.

But we're *unconscious* when we decide to buy a new car on top of our existing $30,000 in credit-card debt. We're unconscious when we buy one more painting or bracelet or condo or stock that we don't need—and then see its value plummet inside of six months. And we're unconscious when a brochure so catches our eye that we purchase a $5,000 cruise to the Caribbean, even though we not long ago returned from another trip and may not have any vacation days or cash left. In other words, we are unconscious about money *when we have no idea how we got into our current financial situation.*

Few things are so precisely calculated and yet so imprecisely understood as money. This much, though, is clear: When we know how, when, where, and why we use our money, we take control. We become conscious about it.

How Unconscious Are We?

Just how unconscious are we with money? Unconsciousness is not in short supply. In fact, America may be one of the most money-unconscious places on earth. Consider:

- Ninety percent of divorces are said to be related to financial problems (source: Adrian Furnham and Michael Argyle, *The Psychology of Money*).
- One in 100 households per year will declare personal bankruptcy (*The New York Times*).
- Nearly 70 percent of consumers live from paycheck to paycheck (*The Wall Street Journal*).
- The average household owes more than $8,000 in credit-card balances (Natalie Jenkins, et al., *You Paid How Much for That?*).
- More than 62 percent of Americans retire on annual incomes of below $10,000 (U.S. Census Bureau).
- About 55 percent of all Americans "always or sometimes worry about their money" (*USA Today*).

How We Learn about Money

In most cases, we develop our sense about money in the same way as we learned about romance: through mimicry and experimentation. We watched what Mom and Dad, or movie actors, or friends did romantically, but we had very little formal training in the art of love. Similarly, we fumbled through flirting, courting, and consummating our relationship with money. Sometimes we got smart about it and developed a satisfactory relationship. At other times, money became a difficult partner—demanding and unforgiving, mercurial. Here today, blown tomorrow.

Money Games are the ways we handle ourselves with money. We all play these games—and *need* to—because they help structure our lives and shape how we live with ourselves and others. Some games are healthy; others are destructive.

We may regularly play the Safety Game, for instance, saving and scrimping for a solid retirement, just like good old Dad did. We may also play the Got-More Game precisely because Dad didn't save and ended up broke.

We may live the Workaholic Game for forty years, earning every penny of our money through toil and tears and hard work rarely punctuated by a vacation. We may wake up every day to the Bag Lady Game, chronically fearing money annihilation at any moment. Or, if we are fortunate, we may play the Simplify Game, where we finally learn to manage our money instead of letting it manage us.

Conscious or Unconscious?

But we can play these games either consciously or unconsciously. If we play them consciously, we can feel good about our decisions. We can sleep peacefully and not fear so much for tomorrow. If we play them unconsciously, they sometimes play us. We become victims, angry partners, failed investors, mistrustful parents, and bitter retirees.

What's the difference between conscious or unconscious play? We know, for example, we need to own a home. So we make the conscious choice to make a down payment and commit to a mortgage. We may *not* know, however, how or why we ended up with an ocean-view, four-bedroom split-level across from the golf course with a jumbo loan and a tax bill that nearly crushes us.

We *consciously* decided to buy a house. But we executed the plan *unconsciously* because of psychological drivers like status, fear, manipulation, ragged self-esteem, or plain old guilt. Those shadowy reasons can leave us scratching our heads or even heading for bankruptcy before we can get to the first tax writeoff of that big house.

It's all in the way we play. We often play our Money Games on an automatic, unaware level. Many of us do what our parents did. We learned our games at their knees, just as they learned from their parents. Maybe we also glean some of the game rules from CNN stock reports, financial analysts, and personal-finance magazines. Or maybe we hone our knowledge of the art of the deal by watching the rich, the famous, and the incarcerated. And we get good at accumulating credit-card debt and assuming ever-bigger mortgages. We learn how to be a player.

But have we also learned how not to be played? Have we learned how to use money consciously, not unconsciously? Here's the premise of this book: We can proceed in mindless ways, shocked when the stock market oscillates, reeling or rejoicing when the economy turns up or down, and elated or deflated when we tally up our yearly income-tax bill. *Or,* we can explore our behavior with money and take our power back. We can learn how to make money decisions that help, not hinder, us. We can understand how money produces healthy or unhealthy relationships with family and friends, and whether it provides us with self-esteem or self-torture.

This is a conscious book. It outlines not only the philosophy of how we get, use, and give money, but also how money plays into the game of our own lives. The book seeks to help us become *real* with what and why we do what we do with money. Learning about our Money Games can make us smarter and help us to stop cheating ourselves. It can inspire us to stop lying and start telling ourselves the truth. And it can assist us in getting real with others, with getting down-to-earth with what we want and what we are willing to do—and not do—to get money.

Above all, understanding the Money Games—and the plays, players, and antidotes—will give us conscious power. It will help put money into service for meeting our conscious needs, rather than putting us into service to meet the demands of our money.

Part I

Why We Play

Chapter One

Why Do You Do What You Do with Money?

Two thousand years ago, your ancestor's net worth might have consisted of a herd of goats. When he went to town, he took his bank account on hooves with him. There he bartered, trading goats for food, property—maybe even a mate—and anything else he needed to get by. He led a plain, simple life, one with clear values and resources.

Money is much more complex today. In fact, it's not wrong to say that it really is what makes the world go 'round. Globally, money shapes national agendas, creates conflicts and wars, spurs innovation, and spawns injustice and oppression as well as diversion and delight. Especially in America, it permeates our lives, affecting not only how we relate to that person on the other side of the bed but also to that person on the other side of the world. A terrorist bombing a continent away or an anthrax-laced letter on the other side of the country can decrease our net worth in minutes.

Money is endemic to almost everything. It's not that human beings haven't always been greedy or materialistic in some sense; what has changed is that money itself—as an instrument and as a concept—now enters into almost every facet of life. You can hardly do anything without, in some way, facing the issue of money. We're no

3

longer concerned with just getting enough money to sustain life; we also worry about leveraging debt, paying for college, seeing our real estate appreciate, getting a handle on long-term debt, balancing fixed and soft assets, nurturing our IRAs and 401(k)s, learning about Fannie Maes and Freddie Macs, bolstering shareholder value, deciding about offshore bank accounts; and paying for our daughter's wedding, our dad's cancer treatment, and our mom's retirement care.

We juggle car depreciation, balloon payments, tax writeoffs, insider trading, the impact of global warming on grain sales, and the effect of oil embargos and suicide bombers on energy prices. Further, instead of just being paid in cash, we may get stock, stock options, or fringe benefits. And instead of just being paid by an employer, we may get our money from rental property, trust funds, annuities, gold futures, and many, many other places. And there's not a herd of goats in sight.

The Root of All Money

Initially, people didn't need money. They subsisted on the land and what nature offered. Mankind was self-sufficient, and we adjusted our lives to the whims of nature and its weather patterns. Then we began to trade with each other.

We shifted from complete dependency on the earth to human interdependency, and that gave rise to money. The ancients found it was easier to count out coins than to make all exchanges in goats or chickens. For example, someone with ten head of cattle to sell may have needed to buy only a small amount of corn. So in return he got future credits (coins) that he could cash later for what he'd need. The coinage system replaced pure barter and introduced to the world the joys—and travails—of money.

Money is now a complex social convention with myriad factors that color how we use, view, and value it. As such, it's become a pervasive force that represents so much power or weakness, control or capitulation, peace or anxiety, and the many shades in between. When we have money, most of us feel powerful. We are aware of the potency of a platinum card, a Porsche, or a pile of hundreds. Money generally brings us respect. It opens doors. It gets us relationships—with banks, stores, car dealerships, insurance companies, mates—and permeates our personal dealings with partners, clients, colleagues, children, parents, pharmacists, grocery store clerks, gas station attendants, and even ourselves.

In fact, as a measure of self-worth and power in our modern culture, money has no rival. Nothing looks more like success than a red Ferrari or an estate in the Hamptons. So when we get money, we usually feel good about our worth, our success, our power, and our future. Conversely, when don't get it, we may feel a lack of power, lowered self-worth, and a limited future. So money stands for some perceived value.

But does money itself actually have any sort of value or power? Does a lowly dime sitting on a table have the power to drive a decision, make or break a deal, bring peace of mind, or cause a world war? A dime alone is basically inert, without much significance. Put that one dime together with millions of others, however, and whole cities can be built. Retract those millions of dimes and people go bankrupt, lose their cars, their homes, maybe even their way of life. Thus, the great power of the lowly dime is due in no small part to not only the value we bestow upon it, but also the rich mystique surrounding this thing we call money.

The Last Taboo

Money is one of our last cultural taboos. Death, sex, relationships, and addictions have been studied and debated. In fact, they have become a staple of afternoon TV talk shows. But while Freud and others have theorized about the place of money in society, you and I seldom talk about it in the course of our day-to-day dealings. We rarely discuss it much even with people we know well, and it certainly isn't a topic for polite dinner conversation.

Why is money such a taboo?

We love money winners in our society. Money failure, however, can trigger some nasty reactions. We tend to stigmatize those without money. And even when we have lots of money, many of us want to hide it, hoard it, bank it, and above all, not let others know we have it. And when we don't have it, we just remain quiet.

We don't particularly like others to know our money secrets. We flinch at having our finances examined lest others see through us. Or want a handout. Or ridicule our financial mishaps. Our tax accountants and CPAs have become this era's priests. It's only to them we confess our financial sins. With money, we become vulnerable. To disclose our net worth opens us up to uncomfortable scrutiny.

In my work with both financial and family clients, I have learned that most people are reluctant to talk about their money lives, their assets, their debts, their money practices, their money beliefs, or their money secrets unless they see a strong benefit in doing so. In fact, many clients will tell me their sex problems before they'll disclose their net worth. And sociologists tell us that couples often are more comfortable divulging to each other the details of their prior sex lives than they are sharing the intimacies of finance.

Talking about personal money practices leaves many of us exposed, vulnerable to the judgments of others. It also opens up the possibility of stopping our Money Games, thus stripping us of our methods for surviving with our money tension.

Because money remains a psychological territory we don't talk about easily, it retains uncommon power. Money has that power because of the emotions, beliefs, and cultural mores we attach to it. We act on those beliefs—many unspoken, many unchallenged, and many handed down in families and cultures—in the ways we interact with money. In many cases, we had to adopt our family's Money Games as children simply to survive. These ways of acting became the adult Money Games we now play, consciously or unconsciously.

Maggie and Bill: Keeping Money Secrets

Take Maggie and Bill, who came to see me to discuss what investments to place in a trust fund they were drawing up for each of their adult children from previous marriages. Both in their early forties, Maggie and Bill had been married for about a year, a second marriage for both. They were excited about their relationship and hopeful for its future. They described a romantic courtship, and long weekends away during their first year of marriage. Both giggled about how compatible they were emotionally and sexually.

Then I asked them about their money. The couple shifted uncomfortably in their chairs. Bill hesitated, but spoke first. He described a variety of funds and investments he was using to pay for his son's graduate school tuition, his business expansion, and spousal support. Maggie's mouth dropped open, however, when Bill also shared that he was maintaining a real estate investment with his ex-wife, Leslie, as co-owner in an apartment building in Arizona.

After a somewhat heated discussion between the two, Maggie settled down and began to detail her financial picture. She described a modest portfolio that included some stocks and mutual funds but no other significant savings. What also came out in the discussion was that she had given two credit cards to her eighteen-year-old daughter in Maggie's name. The two cards were now maxed out at $10,000 each, and Maggie, unbeknownst to Bill, was slowly paying off the bills out of her modest office manager's income, while Maggie's daughter continued to party and charge away at college.

It was Bill's turn to be furious. By the end of the meeting, both Maggie and Bill had scooted their chairs away from each other. They sat scowling, arms folded, accusing each other of lying about his or her money practices. This couple's money secrets were already driving them apart.

As I mentioned, sometimes the Money Games we play are conscious, sometimes not. Bill, for example, had made a conscious choice not to disclose all of his real estate holdings to Maggie because "I didn't think she needed to know all of the complexities." Unconsciously, though, Bill probably was playing a series of games in order to maintain control over Maggie, their relationship, and his money.

Maggie hadn't disclosed her true financial picture to Bill because "my relationship with my daughter is between us." She and Bill were involved in what they thought was a co-equal relationship, but they were attempting to live secret, parallel financial lives. That's a recipe for disaster. How does this happen?

Money Games are how we meet our needs and align our belief systems. In fact, much of the confusion we experience in our lives with money stems from living with conflicted money beliefs. Out of loyalty to our parents, we may still honor their beliefs with money. Yet as adults we now have beliefs that may run counter to those that we learned as kids. We do our best to integrate these conflicting beliefs and make them manageable. But this cauldron of conflicting money beliefs, values, and attitudes creates an internal struggle that shows up in our Money Games.

Money Needs and Behavior

There is no one-size-fits-all approach to figuring out how we deal with money. Few of us behave in prescribed ways. Once our emotions with money are triggered, all bets are off. We start randomly trying out Money Games, seeking the one that will stop the current money discomfort. If the discomfort is too much for us, we may spiral down into an unhealthy money-coping mechanism, or addiction.

Why did Bill keep his financial relationship with his ex-wife hidden from Maggie? Bill says he just "never considered I'd do it any other way, and that's my business. My financial decisions—and my past—are my own." Why did Maggie "neglect" to tell Bill about the credit-card debt? "My daughter is my business," she says, "and I need to help her because she's a poor student with no support from her father." Both had kept financial secrets for what they thought were sound reasons. But the reality is that their personal fears and mistrust were driving a wedge between them. Consciously they felt they were being independent and autonomous. Unconsciously, each was operating out of a Money Game they probably had been playing with people for years.

Where Our Needs Come From

Where do our money needs come from? An easy way to understand the psychology behind Money Games is to learn a little about Abraham Maslow's hierarchy of needs. In the 1940s, Maslow, a well-known psychologist, theorized that whatever a person needs at the moment affects his or her motivation, priorities, and behavior. A need creates tension, Maslow said. And the behavior that follows seeks to reduce that tension or discomfort. These needs are often unconscious, culturally induced, and societally endorsed.

Maslow also believed that people have an internal need pushing them toward self-actualization (fulfillment) and personal superiority. However, he suggested we tend to meet lower-level needs before we can focus on higher ones and progress to self-actualization. Maslow's hierarchy shows these need levels and resultant behaviors. Here's how he constructed his hierarchy:

self-actualization

ego status, esteem belonging
social activity

safety, security

basic physiological needs

Physiological and survival needs (food, water, shelter, warmth) are the base of our money-needs priorities. With regard to money, these show up in being able to have enough money to put food on the table, pay the mortgage, and, in general, survive day to day.

Safety needs (security, stability, freedom from fear) form the next tier and include our money practices of saving, making prudent investments, buying modest homes and cars, and stockpiling enough money to offset potential losses.

Belonging and social needs (friends, family, spouse, lover relationships) form the next level. Financially, these needs appear in how we use money to join groups, socialize and get friends, influence family relationships, and how we give money to charities or church organizations.

Esteem and ego status needs (achievement, mastery, recognition, respect) are met with money spent for things like personalized license plates, trendy cars and clothes, more upscale houses, and publicized financial success.

Self-actualization needs (pursuit of inner talent, creativity, and fulfillment) are addressed with financial actions that involve personal growth. This might include further education, personal growth efforts, and contributions to societal and/or global health initiatives. These are acts that are motivated by what's best for many as opposed to just one's self-interest.

None of these needs is wrong or bad, or better than others. As human beings, we may all operate out of each of these need areas at various times in our lives. But we get into financial distress when we operate unconsciously out of chronically unbalanced needs, or struggle with competing needs.

To better understand our primary money needs, let's turn the pyramid on its side and look at it another way. If we attach priorities to our money needs, a system of values emerges. For example, some of us are more motivated by social expressions of our money and also the personal recognition we get for it. We may be minimally interested in self-actualization and gaining self-esteem, but may be deeply concerned with joining others in common causes out of a need to belong. Our money-needs profile might look like this:

Sample Allotment of Money Needs	
Physiological survival	10%
Safety	10%
Belonging/Social	50%
Esteem/Ego status	25%
Self-actualization	5%

Our primary money need in this case is belonging/social with a secondary focus on esteem/ego status. With this money-need priority, we probably join groups, giving our time and money to participate in teams and gain acceptance. As a secondary need, this profile suggests we'd like to be recognized for our money status. So perhaps we drive a very nice car to these team events and have groups over to our lavish home for parties and dress so as to bring attention to ourselves. We are probably more into spending than saving, and we don't think too much about acting responsibly with money, such as having a detailed retirement plan in place at this point.

This doesn't mean these needs priorities can't change. In fact, they do, according to your stage of life development (young adult, single young adult, young married, early child rearing, adolescent child rearing, young adult launching, middle age, old age), job change, physical health, religious practices, and many other factors.

Neil and Janelle: Conflicting Priorities

Let's explore money needs more closely by taking a look at Neil and Janelle. Neil is in his early thirties, unmarried, and plays for a professional sports team as a fringe player. He sometimes travels with the team and often coordinates with local media about the games and the team interviews. Neil has chosen to keep a modest rental apartment near the beach, invests in no-load mutual funds, dates periodically, but has no long-range plans to marry or start a family. Neil's money needs chart looks like this:

High Belonging/Social Needs	
Physiological survival	10%
Safety	5%
Belonging/Social	55%
Esteem/Ego status	20%
Self-actualization	10%

With a profile similar to the sample given above, right now Neil has low survival, safety, and self-actualization needs, but high belonging needs. With regard to money, that means that Neil focuses his resources on being part of the team atmosphere. He buys and wears team clothing and hats, and he keeps his financial entanglements low and uncomplicated. He works out with some teammates at the local fitness club. He takes fairly expensive biking and hiking travel outings with various groups, and he maintains close ties with family members, who live about a hundred miles away. At Christmas, the family lavishes each other with gifts and usually takes some kind of skiing vacation together. Neil's savings are modest and usually he spends most of his paycheck on sports outings, group activities, and being social in general. Neil's father works in real estate and drives a flashy Lexus. Neil's mother, an event planner, conducts her business while driving an SUV. None of the family has ever worried particularly about money, but Neil's father is always looking for the next million-dollar sale.

During a ski trip, Neil meets Janelle, twenty-eight, on the slopes. She's on a ski trip with her company, a major accounting firm. She's been a junior accountant with the firm since leaving college and is working her way up the ranks. She is prudent with her money, having watched her father go bankrupt during the 1980s because of sudden changes in the tax laws that affected limited partnerships. At that time, the family lost its ranch-style house, and her father's retirement savings were used to pay creditors. Shaken, Janelle's father went back to work as a mid-level engineer. After being depressed for a year, Janelle's mother returned to nursing to work in assisted-living care. Janelle remembers having to sew her own clothes and take part-time jobs through high school to help make ends meet.

Currently Janelle owns her condo, drives a modest Hyundai, has a large savings account, and maintains a solid, diversified mutual-funds portfolio. She owns a modest portfolio of utilities and consumer-staples stocks, but she is always careful not to invest more than 20 percent of her money in volatile issues. Janelle has a few close, trusted friends but enjoys socializing in sports situations. She has thought of getting married and starting a family, but she wants to wait not only for the right person, but also for the right time, to be financially prepared. Janelle's chart looks like this:

High Safety Need	
Physiological survival	20%
Safety	50%
Belonging/Social	10%
Esteem/Ego status	10%
Self-actualization	10%

Janelle's money needs reflect an emphasis on safety. She also shows a fairly high priority on physiological and survival needs. These kinds of needs are reflected in her cautious, prudent approach to money. Janelle values saving money and checks her balance frequently. She is cautious with investments, and thinks very hard before she rewards herself with things she deems frivolous, like shopping sprees or jewelry. Spending money to look good, belong, or self-actualize are fairly low on her priority list, although she does enjoy sports with others.

Neil and Janelle fall madly in love on the slopes, get engaged, and then marry six months later. Within a year, Janelle finds out she's expecting, and the couple's idyllic first year of marriage starts to become a battleground. Their money-needs priorities are coming into conflict.

Neil realizes he must start thinking about what it means to be a father. Though they've already given up his apartment and have been living in Janelle's condo, he immediately begins looking to lease a three-bedroom house with an ocean view. He cuts back on his outings with "the boys," stops taking ski and hiking vacations, takes a part-time marketing job during the off-season, and puts a down payment on an Eddie Bauer SUV that can seat a family of six. This gives him vague discomfort because owning all this "stuff" seems "really foreign" to him and he misses his team buddies. But he does it anyway. He's about to become a family man, and he's going to be the best father he can be.

Janelle, on the other hand, is horrified at what Neil has done with the down payment she thought they had earmarked for a modest home in the suburbs about twenty miles out of town. She thought their five-year-old cars would work just fine for the early years while the baby was small. She is aghast that Neil wants her now to sell the condo and use the money on a big home and loads of furniture, instead of investing it in a more modest property she feels they can afford.

But after a few sleepless nights, she reluctantly agrees. She withdraws $20,000 from her savings and stock sales, and agrees to use it for a house but demands it be in a modest neighborhood.

When Neil drives home the next Saturday all smiles and braggadocio, Janelle takes one look at the expensive SUV and goes to bed for two days, tired and depressed.

Money Tension

Neil and Janelle's story illustrates the internal and external money tensions that arise when needs conflict. *Internal money tension* surfaces when basic needs collide and compete for attention within ourselves. In Neil's case, his dominant money need as a single man was belonging/social. As a soon-to-be family man, however, a secondary need, esteem and ego status, surfaced due to his new role and what he'd picked up from his own family. He had learned from parents, family, friends, and his culture in general that a new father should take certain actions with money. He dutifully complied, though his gut presented him with vague dissatisfaction and disorientation— internal money tension. In fact, he developed an ulcer as a result of self-induced warfare that has him fighting for his own beliefs regarding money versus his beliefs assimilated from childhood.

For Janelle, her primary money need—safety—was also shifting. It was shifting to accommodate the survival needs of her new family. Her previously secondary driver of physiological/survival needs began to compete with her primary safety need, causing her internal money fear and tension. She became depressed, probably triggered by the thoughts of terror she experienced as a child when her family went bankrupt and lost its home. She feared she and Neil might be following in her father's footsteps.

For Neil and Janelle together, their external money tension took the form of conflict and competing agendas. This tension, coupled with the stresses and normal strains of a new marriage, impending parenthood, and financial restructuring around a family, caused the pair to begin to fight openly. Each accused the other of undermining the marriage. But what was going on at a more basic level was a clash of personality and wills. Its theme: Whose family beliefs, values, and attitudes with money would prevail?

Janelle accused Neil of being irresponsible. Neil called Janelle "tight and paranoid." Both wondered aloud whether the other would be any good as a parent. Without a conscious understanding of how their tension was playing itself out, Neil and Janelle saw their relationship deteriorate into arguing, exhaustion, anxiety, and anger. The indirect payoff of the conflict was the initial rush, increased sexual arousal (and "makeup sex" after fighting), and momentary drawing together in the form of brief intimacy. But the downside was the crumbling of the relationship overall and another step backward in their communication.

We'll return to Neil and Janelle's story later, but now let's take a look at your money-needs profile. Before going on to Chapter 2, be sure to take and score the following assessment to come up with your dominant and secondary money needs.

Your Money-Needs Profile Assessment

Put a check mark on the blank line at the end of any question where a *yes* response would apply to you more than 50 percent of the time:

1. Do you currently have or strive for complete financial independence so you will have the freedom to live your life as you like? (V) ____
2. Do you enjoy being a financial leader or knowledgeable expert? (W) ____
3. Do you stay in touch with family, business associates, and friends often via phone, e-mail, letters, and face-to-face encounters? (X) ____
4. Do you like to know the financial rules in any situation? (Y) ____
5. Do you avoid financial risk taking? (Z) ____
6. Do you continue to educate yourself? (V) ____
7. Do you like to share your stories of financial success? (W) ____

8. Do you seek a level playing field so that no one else has an unfair advantage over you in your money dealings? (X) _____

9. Do you insist on having money in your savings account at all times? (Y) _____

10. Do you spend a lot of your day worrying if you will have enough money for food, rent, and clothes? (Z) _____

11. Do you like to choose how, when, and where you spend your income? (V) _____

12. Do you like finding ways out of tough financial situations? (W) _____

13. Do you prefer the group—not you—be recognized for good financial work? (X) _____

14. Do you feel the need to have a secure retirement income? (Y) _____

15. Do you keep your dollars fairly liquid and accessible at a moment's notice? (Z) _____

16. Do you regularly give of your time and money to worthy causes? (V) _____

17. Do you enjoy financial risk taking? (W) _____

18. Are you more apt to invest because others are doing it rather than take an investment risk on your own? (X) _____

19. Are you determined to have your credit card carry no balance and is being debt free one of your burning goals? (Y) _____

20. Do you feel you aren't smart enough to be proficient at managing your finances? (Z) _____

21. Do you seek out financial answers? (V) _____

22. Do you enjoy making deals? (W) _____

23. Do you build and maintain a current list of business and financial contacts? (X) _____

24. Do you have health insurance that covers every possibility? (Y) _____

25. Do you have trouble sometimes trusting yourself and other people financially? (Z) _____

26. Do you prefer to work alone rather than in teams or groups? (V) _____

27. Do you usually give to financial causes only because you think they are worth it? (W) _____

28. Do you prefer to work in teams and groups rather than alone? (X) _____

29. Do you live in a gated or guarded community? (Y) _____

30. Do you have dollars stashed in several places for ready access? (Z) _____

31. Do you enjoy teaching or coaching others regarding money and resources? (V) _____

32. Do you daydream about what life would be like if you were rich or, if you are already rich, if you had even more money? (W) _____

33. Have you been part of a financial or investments group or do you have plans to join one in the future? (X) _____

34. Would you sacrifice buying the car you really wanted in order to buy a really safe car you or your partner felt you should have instead? (Y) _____

35. Do you studiously avoid the stock market because of the financial risk? (Z) _____

36. Do you prefer to live and let live with regard to money? (V) _____

37. Have you given dollars or volunteered service particularly to receive recognition? (W) _____

38. Do you prefer mutual funds so you don't have to monitor individual stocks? (X) _____

39. Do you feel panicky when you lose your job or your income stream? (Y) _____

40. Do you handle your money pretty much the same way your grandparents did? (Z) _____

41. Have you learned to be tolerant of your financial failures and successes? (V) _____

42. Do you like to be a big winner with stocks, real estate, or other investments? (W) _____

43. Do you ever ease your guilt with family members by giving money, gifts, or trips to compensate for time away from loved ones? (X) _____

44. Do you feel particularly uneasy when you have less than $5,000 in the bank? (Y) ____

45. Do you regularly clip coupons, look only for bargains, and buy mostly things on sale? (Z) ____

46. Do you have a hobby or second career that is independent of your need to make money? (V) ____

47. Do you feel a need to impress others with your wealth? (W) ____

48. Would buying your parents a brand-new home be one of the first things you'd do with a million dollars? (X) ____

49. Do you know your family history and enjoy living near family? (Y) ____

50. Do you wear clothes that are sometimes past their prime, looking somewhat threadbare or scuffed? (Z) ____

51. Do you tend to use credit sparingly? (V) ____

52. Do you have a large (more than $5,000) total credit-card debt? (W) ____

53. Do you feel obligated to give to your church or favorite charitable organization because others pressure you to give? (X) ____

54. Do you ever have fears or nightmares about being homeless, out on the street, or being penniless? (Y) ____

55. Do you typically blame your partner for the financial problems in your family? (Z) ____

56. Do you devote more of your dollars to self-improvement rather than the acquisition of things? (V) ____

57. Do you more often acquire things because you want them rather than need them? (W) ____

58. Can you admit that part of you married for money, financial security, or because you thought your spouse had good earning potential? (X) ____

59. Do you worry about not being able to pay the rent or mortgage? (Y) ____

60. Do you live from paycheck to paycheck, rarely having much left over for nonessentials? (Z) ____

61. Do you consider work as a medium of expression rather than a paycheck source? (V) ____

62. Do you have a fear that you are not as financially adequate as your friend or colleague? (W) ____

63. Is there financial jealousy between you and your partner (when one of you makes more than the other or gets a better raise)? (X) ____

64. Do you worry regularly about losing your job, your house, not getting a raise, and not getting promoted? (Y) ____

65. Have you and/or your partner had to work two or more jobs for more than one year to make ends meet? (Z) ____

66. Do you organize your financial goals so that whatever is necessary and sufficient has first priority, rather than items that could demonstrate your wealth? (V) ____

67. Do you feel a need to sometimes compete for financial superiority with friends, colleagues, or family members? (W) ____

68. Do you sometimes encourage loved ones to "charge whatever you want" in order to preserve the relationship? (X) ____

69. Do you judge people who spend a lot of dollars for present pleasures and short-term goals as being unwise and insecure? (Y) ____

70. Have you ever had a relative or close friend lose everything financially and worry that the same might happen to you? (Z) ____

Scoring

Add up the number of boxes you checked according to the letter following each statement. For example, count how many *Z* statements you checked and place that number on the appropriate line below. Continue until you have added all categories.

Self-actualization (V):   ____   Safety/Security (Y):   ____
Ego Status/Esteem (W): ____   Physiological survival (Z): ____
Belonging/Social (X):   ____

The assessment includes fourteen questions for each of these five categories of money needs. The numbers you write next to each category will give you a general idea of how important each need is to you. An 11 or 12 next to "Safety/Security," for example, could indicate that you have a cautious attitude toward money and life, similar to that of Janelle, the accountant profiled above. You can also examine your above scores to see which categories of needs are not that important in your life right now.

Chapter Two

Money Games People Play

Every day we spend, keep, save, invest, or otherwise decide what to do about money. This takes up a lot of time and psychological energy. As Joe Dominguez, author (*Your Money or Your Life*) and financial analyst, pointed out, one way or another, we exchange a big chunk of our lives for money.

Much of this energy, whether destructive or productive, ends up becoming the dynamic of the Money Games. These games keep us numb and distracted and prevent us from getting what we really want out of life: happiness and fulfillment.

We talk ourselves into believing we will become happy if we win the game. But someone keeps moving the finish line. We run and run and never seem to be satisfied.

When we play Money Games unconsciously, we lose touch with reality and our true selves. We get caught up in situations that require us to navigate around underground beliefs in order to feel comfortable. Such subconscious behaviors with money are a short-term fix that eventually must be dealt with either through mounting debts or through money secrets that can destroy relationships. We need to consider whether the psychological cost ultimately leaves us in the red or the black.

But when we can be straightforward about our money behavior, we use less energy. We become more aware of the Money Games we play and understand how our lack of responsibility with money hurts us rather than helps us win.

The Origins of Money Games

Some 1,500 years ago, we didn't play Money Games. So we have to ask ourselves: What was different back then? First, we lived in small communities where maybe we raised goats, another neighbor raised cattle, and yet another grew vegetables. We were at one with nature, dependent on what it provided us. There was community, because we could not have survived without each other's assistance. What we grew and raised was shared with little waste. The milk from the goats and the meat from the cattle nourished us. The hides from the cattle and the goats clothed us, and the food we grew fed the animals as well as us. Everything had a use.

Then perhaps a nomad happened by, and we saw his fine clothes and ax. We wondered out loud where he acquired these goods, and he replied, "All of the villagers in my land meet once a month and exchange goods." At these marketplaces, personal desires and feelings of separateness and self-interest first surfaced. We began thinking about how our own children might need new clothes or how our mates might look in a new robe.

We originally intended to make sure everyone in our community had his or her basic needs met. A secondary aim was to share excesses with each other (so we could then spend them as we saw fit). What went wrong? Individuals began to see there were benefits to be gained. And if they worked harder or faster at tasks like harvesting, why shouldn't they directly benefit from their efforts and keep a bigger share of the pie? Money Games grew as individuals learned how to get more out of their neighbors at less expense to themselves.

Soon, one tribesman's time or product or service became more valuable than another's. There were "winners" and "losers." We began to ignore those who were having difficulty surviving so we could enjoy the fruits of our own labors. We became less conscious of the community's needs. We started maneuvering with our resources to justify our self-interest. We drifted away from our true life purpose, which includes communal responsibility.

We swapped the good of all for the good of ourselves. We moved from a global perspective to an individual mind-set. As mentioned earlier, this is also when coins came into being. When we had surplus goods, tokens (coins) were issued so we could use these tokens as exchange for future needs. People then agreed to pay us extra tokens for letting them use our coins when we didn't need them, and this became banking. As we moved from wholeness or oneness to being self-focused, the games became more crafty. Over the ages, we evolved a complex, global system of trading, saving, lending, spending, leveraging, and investing.

Back to Maggie and Bill

Now let's fast-forward to the present day and to the example of Maggie and Bill from Chapter 1. Bill was paying a price for hiding from his new wife Maggie his financial dealings with his ex-wife. Let's say that on a scale of 1 to 10 (with 10 being complete ease), Bill is a 9 on being comfortable with the need to hide his assets, and a 3 with not being open with Maggie. If so, he is in alignment with his current money belief system. He can live with not being honest with Maggie (and the fallout when she finds out) *because it's more important for him to have financial autonomy and safety.*

Maggie, on the other hand, may believe that for them to have a successful marriage, Bill needs to break off his financial relationships with his ex-wife (a 10 on her scale of must-have financial trust). Otherwise, she may threaten to divorce him.

Thus, we see the couple's Money Games in conflict. Both are playing the Mistrust Game, among others. If Bill discovers that his love for Maggie and his need to make their marriage work is, in fact, *at least as important as his money safety needs,* then he may be ready to come clean with himself and her. He may then be able to compromise to get his core needs—money safety *and* a trusting marriage—met.

Maggie, for her part, has a different dynamic working. Her father ran everything in the household and didn't give women any voice. So she grew up thinking men had all the financial answers. Now, trying to be a good parent, she gives her daughter everything she wants. Maggie fears that if she tells Bill about that, he'll veto her largesse. She won't have a say, and she'll end up being both a bad parent and treated as a child by Bill. She won't be entirely healthy until she can be honest with her husband in their financial affairs.

Maneuvers Become Money Games

It's human and natural to want to get our needs met. But money tension comes bubbling up from our subconscious when our soul's blueprint (our centered selves) conflicts with the way we're living our life. These money tensions play themselves out in Money Games. These games are nothing more than defense mechanisms to protect us from a way of life that is contrary to what is best for us. In Bill and Maggie's case, each plays the Mistrust Game because they're both hiding a behavior they're uncomfortable with but can't yet confront.

Think of a Money Game as a circuit breaker that is activated so we don't blow our central-nervous-system fuse. By playing the game, we are able to experiment with our money consciousness in a less destructive way. When we play Money Games, we can take one of two paths. The first is to ignore the results of the game and how we feel about it; in this case we play the game(s) until we die and never learn or grow. The second is to notice the feelings the game generates, examine the game, and when valuable lessons are revealed to us, use the knowledge to direct us back to our true life purpose. From this path, we grow and thrive.

Until we have mastered our Money Games, we simply cannot live in concert with both our money and our soul. Oneness and a global perspective cannot be attained until mastery of our Money

Games shows us how to balance our separate self-interests with common-good interests.

How did it work out for Bill and Maggie? Well, with some help, they were able to come up with a workable solution. Bill continued his real estate dealings with his ex-wife for a while, but with two important changes: First, he came up with a plan that would allow their financial partnership to be dissolved as soon as real estate values permitted. Second, Maggie would attend the meetings between Bill and his ex-wife, so she could see that nothing was being done behind her back. As for Maggie and her daughter, Bill would be brought into the loop and be told what was being contemplated. He'd be encouraged to offer his opinion, though the final decision was Maggie's.

In both cases, they ceased their maneuvering and did what they had to do out in the open. Your maneuverings become your Money Games when those maneuverings become an established pattern. And why do they become an established pattern? Because for you they work.

Games become an intricate coping mechanism for keeping tension low and maintaining peace—until your cover is blown, of course. Depending on how great the tension, we use varying types of coping strategies and resultant games with often escalating results. Sometimes we subconsciously blow our covers when we have mastered a specific Money Game. Then we select from the myriad other Money Games we keep in our quiver, and a new game begins.

Using the two couples we've discussed, let's take a closer look at their money needs, range of coping strategies, and the Money Games they've learned to play with themselves and their partners (the games mentioned will be described in detail in the chapters that follow).

Bill

- **Life stage**—Middle age, postdivorce financial stress, second marriage, adult child launching, planning for retirement
- **Money beliefs, values, expectations**—Money control, money

status and ego gratification, planning for the future, financial planning for children, separate financial identities

- **Primary money need**—Esteem/ego status; **Secondary need**—Safety
- **Initial coping strategies**—Takes parental approach with others toward money, maintains control through open or hidden means, shows off money through status symbols (multiple properties, cars)
- **Escalated coping strategies**—Colludes with outside parties to maintain control of money; hides money or investments; makes changes as needed to his will to accommodate personal relationships
- **Games played**—Money and Sex Game, Social Climber Game, Mistrust Game

Maggie

- **Life stage**—Early middle age, postdivorce financial stress, second marriage, adult child, late launching due to parental overattachment, not planning for retirement
- **Money beliefs, values, expectations**—Money as status and love, men as primary breadwinner, men (husband) pay for her financial future, overinvolvement with children as evidence of good parenting, debt as shame and must be hidden, lack of financial control and responsibility
- **Primary money need**—Esteem/ego status; **Secondary need**—Belonging/social
- **Initial coping strategies**—Takes adolescent approach to money responsibility by spending today and worrying tomorrow, uses mild manipulation, gives guilt to others by making gifts with strings, hides behavior for fear of punishment
- **Escalated coping strategies**—Accumulates more debt in spite, triangulates daughter between herself and new husband, plays "poor me," opens hidden credit card accounts
- **Games played**—Social Climber Game, Mistrust Game

Neil

- **Life stage**—Young adult/new parent
- **Money beliefs, values, expectations**—Evolving money values motivated first by social and family values and second by self-esteem dynamics, believes in stuff as demonstration of responsibility, lives for today and subtly ridicules attempts to plan for financial future
- **Primary money need**—Belonging/social; **Secondary need**—Esteem/ego status
- **Initial coping strategies**—Shows commitment by buying stuff, demonstrates growing ego status need by needing to buy top-of-the-line stuff, gives up social relationships in the interest of the family, denigrates financial planning
- **Escalated coping strategies**—Makes decisions in a vacuum, takes control through calling the financial shots, blames partner
- **Games played**—Social Climber Game, Workaholic Game

Janelle

- **Life stage**—Young adult/new parent
- **Money beliefs, values, expectations**—Evolving money values motivated first by safety needs and second by physiological/survival needs, believes in solid savings and investment plan as demonstration of responsibility, lives for tomorrow and subtly ridicules attempts to live in the now, hyperbelief in financial caution, fear of lacking and financial failure
- **Primary money need**—Safety; **Secondary need**—Physiological/survival
- **Initial coping strategies**—Attempts to maintain control of financial future, parents, and spouse regarding money matters; takes on hyper-responsible role
- **Escalated coping strategies**—Becomes ill under extreme

stress, blocks moving forward, shuts down emotionally, shames partner, overfunctions
- **Games played**—Mistrust Game, Bag Lady Game, Self-Worth Game, Workaholic Game

As seen in the above examples, money actions are usually made within a complex system of beliefs, social learning, and positioning. The couples described here aren't acting much differently than any of us do in times of money stress. It is possible, though, to become conscious of both our money beliefs and Money Games and thus make more enlightened choices about how we interact with ourselves and others around money.

Neil and Janelle, for example, ultimately learned about their money needs and were able to be honest about how they were acting with each other out of extreme discomfort and crisis. They were able to negotiate and get all sets of needs met by sitting down with an objective third party who helped them clarify and resolve their money conflicts. They then worked out a prudent plan of buying a house and planning for their future that was compatible with both Neil's need for belonging and status, and Janelle's need to keep some money in the bank and plan for their financial future.

In this case, though, the compromise took its toll. Janelle initially suppressed her need for safety and surrendered to the more immediate goal of meeting the couple's desire to take care of themselves and the baby. Over time, however, she realized it was too much to give up. The game she was playing with herself was causing too much tension. She was making herself ill over conflicting needs that were playing themselves out in her conflicting decisions.

Quid Pro Quo

Most of us play a sort of quid pro quo Money Game with ourselves. We buy this to get that, invest in one thing to receive another. We are driven by needs and motivations as people, and sometimes it can be difficult to clarify what we really want and what we believe we should want. We can consciously agree to pay a price for what we want and can live with the consequences. Or, if we make decisions on an unconscious basis, we are often surprised at the consequences and stoop to blaming others and hating conditions.

Money Games come in a wide variety. Each game comes with:

- *Beliefs* about money
- *Roles* we play with specific people
- *Rules* we use in specific situations
- *Expectations* we have of ourselves and others when it comes to the specific Money Game
- *Secrets or truths* we have about what we make conscious (real, authentic, known) or unconscious (inauthentic, manipulative, colluding) to ourselves and others

In the following pages, we will explore fifteen key Money Games. How constructive or destructive these games are depends largely on how conscious we are of playing them. If we are comfortable with spending $4,000 on a weekend vacation and can live with the consequences, we are playing a conscious Money Game. We are at peace. If we are uncomfortable with spending $4,000 on the weekend vacation and end up regretting it, we are playing an unconscious, destructive Money Game. At the very least, we are chagrined; at the worst, we are angry, resentful, and guilty.

Here are some of the most common games we play:

1. The More Money Game

Game: Money alleviates worries.
Belief: If I have more money, I'll be happier.

2. The Victim Game

Game: I can't take care of myself, so I will find someone who will.
Belief: I am not capable of supporting myself. If I could, it wouldn't be enough.

3. The Money and Sex Game

Game: Money gets me sex and love.
Belief: My money makes me more attractive than I am.

4. The Workaholic Game

Game: The burden's on me. If I don't produce, we won't eat.
Belief: I have to do it all or they won't love me and I won't be able to forgive myself.

5. The Bag Lady Game

Game: I have to save or I'll be broke before I know it.
Belief: Poverty's just around the corner.

6. The Got-More Game

Game: Whoever has the most stuff, wins.
Belief: If I have more than you, I'm better than you and I have more power than you do.

7. The Old Money Game

Game: I've got money and so I'm entitled.
Belief: I'm better than you since I have inherited money. You owe me respect.

8. The Social Climber Game

Game: If I hang out with the rich, I'll end up rich.
Belief: I can acquire worth and esteem if I rub elbows with the rich.

9. The Self-Worth Game

Game: I am my money. My money makes me who I am.
Belief: With money, I'm somebody. Without money, I have no value.

10. The Kiddo Game

Game: I can always turn to Mom and Dad for money.
Belief: I don't have to take charge of my responsibilities with money since Mom and Dad will bail me out.

11. The Mistrust Game

Game: I can't trust anyone to know about my money dealings—even my partner or my kids.
Belief: I must control my money to feel safe.

12. The Moneyholic Game

Game: I can charge or gamble or buy anything I want. Something will happen to get me out of it.
Belief: I want what I want and I want it now.

13. The Slave Game

Game: I have to endure this awful job for life in order to get money.
Belief: Getting money is a hard sacrifice and I don't deserve any better.

14. The Giving Game

Game: I give from a place of safety and abundance.
Belief: I have more than enough and want to share my abundance.

15. The Simplify Game

Game: I take responsibility for my finances and choose to right-size.
Belief: I want peace of mind, so I am taking charge of my money in a healthy way.

There are, of course, more Money Games and variations and combinations of the games listed above. You now may be ready to explore *your* Money Games. Internally, you may be aware that your clock is ticking and that you have only so much time left on this planet. Thus, you may find you are playing several games at once. You may be overwhelmed. You may be ready to address the roots of your money problems once and for all.

First, please take and score the following assessment. It will give you an idea of which are your preferred games, and which of the following chapters should be of particular interest to you.

Money Games Assessment

Check the statements that sound most like you, then total your check marks on the line at the end of each game.

Game #1

_____ When I have money, I feel less worried.

_____ I believe that if I had more money, I'd be happier.

_____ I think that people who have money are happier than I am.

_____ My parents often wished for more money.

_____ My mother or father sometimes said they wished I could get a career and make lots of money.

_____ I often find myself thinking that if I had more money, everything would be better.

_____ I think I should be making a certain amount of money by a certain age.

_____ I sometimes take big risks to get or earn more money.

_____ I often find myself comparing myself to others regarding how much money we make, what cars we drive, and what homes we own.

_____ I sometimes wake up in a cold sweat, worrying about having enough to pay for something.

Total: _____

Game #2

_____ I feel unknowledgeable about money matters and feel pretty uncomfortable around financial matters in general.

_____ I generally let others manage my money matters for me.

_____ I don't think I can fully take care of myself financially alone.

_____ I feel panicky when I think about money and don't really like to be bothered with it.

_____ My parents usually handled my money for me.

_____ I have been told I am sort of dumb about money.

_____ I have to admit that it's a lot easier to pay someone to handle my money for me.

_____ I get tired of people treating me like a child about money.

_____ I tend to get into relationships where my partner or loved one controls the money.

_____ If I am honest about it, I don't think I can be trusted with money.

Total: _____

Game #3

_____ If I am really honest about it, I sometimes like to impress people whom I am attracted to with my money power.

_____ I find that the more money I demonstrate I have, the better my relationships go.

_____ I fear that others won't like me if I am poor.

_____ I regularly do things to make an impression on others with my clothes, car, house, apartment, stocks, or vacations.

_____ I have had a rocky divorce or end of a relationship that included a lot of financial angst.

_____ My parents often fought over money with each other and I guess I've inherited that tendency.

_____ I feel out of control if my partner has the upper hand in money issues.

_____ I usually let my partner control the money and he or she then lets me spend some portion of that money.

_____ A lot of people consider me sexy because of my financial situation, and frankly I've used that sometimes to get a partner to go out with me, have sex with me, or marry me.

_____ If I am really honest about it, I sometimes give sex to get something else.

Total: _____

Game #4

_____ I feel responsible for my family's financial welfare.

_____ Nobody else can help me with my financial burden.

_____ I put in more than forty hours a week for more than 50 percent of the year.

_____ I sometimes brag to people about how much I work.

_____ I regularly work on the weekends.

_____ I work two jobs.

_____ My partner complains that I work too much.

_____ One or both of my parents worked a lot and I guess I am following suit.

_____ I sometimes resent people because they are so dependent on me.

_____ I have to work hard to get ahead and I have to get ahead no matter what.

Total: _____

Game #5

_____ I fear I may be broke someday.

_____ I have known someone who went broke and it was terrifying.

_____ I have money saved in various places where I can get my hands on it quickly.

_____ I sometimes think the world is a fearful place and that I really have very few alternatives if I get down and out.

_____ Sometimes I wonder if I can really make a good living and wondering makes me feel a little ashamed.

_____ I save almost everything.

_____ I clip coupons as much as I can.

_____ I buy on sale more than 50 percent of the time.

_____ People sometimes call me a pack rat.

_____ I save first, give to others and myself last.

Total: _____

Game #6

_____ I grew up having to compete with others for cash, attention, toys, and other things.

_____ My mom and/or dad used to compete with each other financially.

_____ Keeping up with the Joneses was important in my family.

_____ Privately, I really envy the rich guys.

_____ If I were really honest with myself, I get a kick out of showing others I have more money than they do.

_____ I have been known to brag about my financial success.

_____ I sometimes feel a little off balance, but I feel better when I can show others when and where I have been a success.

_____ I enjoy telling stories about my financial wins.

_____ I hide my financial losses from others.

_____ People should respect me if I make more money than they do.

Total: _____

Game #7

_____ If I am honest about it, my inheritance or large estate makes me feel just a little bit better than others.

_____ I truly feel others should show me respect because of the money I have.

_____ I generally feel more comfortable in society because I have money.

_____ I sometimes wonder how other people make it without inherited money or new wealth.

_____ I was raised to act like our family money entitled us to more than others get.

_____ There are simply some people with less than I have whom I don't want to associate with.

_____ I sometimes wonder if people like me for my money or myself.

_____ I have had one or two experiences where people were nasty to me until they found out I had money.

_____ I usually am able to get anything I want because of my money.

_____ In relationships, I sometimes have been successful only because of my money.

Total: _____

Game #8

_____ I enjoy reading about the up-and-comers and wish I were like them.

_____ I secretly envy my friends or associates when they make it big or score socially.

_____ I have sometimes done things so I could be seen with the right people.

_____ I have relationships with people I don't really like but whom I think can help my career or social position.

_____ I have occasionally dated or married people because of who their parents are.

_____ I sometimes have volunteered or given money just so I could rub elbows with people with more social clout.

_____ I am nervous around socially prominent people and try hard to behave and look acceptable.

_____ My parents were often envious of those with prominence.

_____ If I am really honest about it, I sometimes use people to get ahead even though I don't necessarily like myself when I do it.

_____ I have been known to hide what I earn or where I work so I appear better off.

Total: _____

Game #9

_____ I believe people wouldn't take me seriously without my having some money.

_____ When I didn't have money in my life, I felt a little worthless.

_____ Generally, I value myself according to how much money I make and have.

_____ I have noticed that the more money I have, the more people truly respect me.

_____ I have had experiences where people, like my parents or others, put me down for not having money and it really hurt me.

_____ I find myself noticing when others have money or not and find myself gravitating toward the haves rather than the have-nots.

_____ My parents led me to believe that they'd be more proud of me if I made a good living.

_____ I have been compared unfavorably to others who make more money.

_____ I have friends and colleagues now who probably would drop me as a friend if I lost all my money or my job.

_____ If I am honest about it, I sometimes judge myself according to how much money I have or make.

Total: _____

Game #10

_____ I inherited money so I have never had to earn my own way.

_____ My parents are very generous and give me everything I need.

_____ My family has bailed me out financially at least three times.

_____ Deep down I don't worry about money much because I know my family will always be there financially.

_____ My family sometimes treats me like a financial idiot even though I know a lot.

_____ I can pay other people to know financial things so I can do more fun things.

_____ My family bought me my first car and house so they'd be sure I started out right.

_____ Sometimes I feel smothered by my parents.

_____ I have to admit that sometimes I really resent my family because of the way they throw money at problems.

_____ I sometimes get this empty feeling inside when it comes to money, cars, and houses.

_____ I don't understand why people get so uptight about financial problems.

Total: _____

Game #11

_____ In general, people can't be trusted to know about my finances.

_____ My parents never were upfront with me about money issues and taught me to do likewise.

_____ We have a lot of secrets in our family and not just about money.

_____ I have used or will use a prenuptial agreement before I get married.

_____ I keep one or two financial things from my partner.

_____ Even in my business, I keep some financial secrets to myself.

_____ I have been known to hide things from the IRS on occasion.

_____ I got taken advantage of regarding money issues once or twice, and I will never let it happen again.

_____ I have had bad breakups in relationships or marriages where I felt I lost out financially in a big way.

_____ Sometimes I have been known to hoard things.

Total: _____

Game #12

_____ I think credit cards are made to be used.

_____ I usually buy whatever I want whether I have the cash or not.

_____ I now have or have had over $20,000 in credit-card debt.

_____ I have more than ten revolving-credit cards.

_____ I have been known to go on a shopping binge, coming home loaded with purchases.

_____ When I get stressed, I go shopping.

_____ I watch the home shopping networks and shop online often.

_____ I find gambling and other money pleasures really exciting.

_____ I have problems with my partner about the amount of money I spend.

_____ It depresses me if I can't buy something new.

Total: _____

Game #13

_____ I work really hard despite the fact that I don't much like my job.

_____ My parents taught me to work hard and stop complaining.

_____ I have been known to work two jobs just so I could buy something special for my family.

_____ I rarely buy anything special for myself.

_____ If I really admit it, I find myself complaining about my job, my boss, and my colleagues more times than not.

_____ I have some career dreams, but I have had to resign myself to the fact that I am pretty much in this job for the duration.

_____ I generally feel good that I work so hard and sacrifice so much.

_____ My parents punished themselves a lot.

_____ My parents punished me a lot.

_____ My parents often told me how much they did for me or gave up to raise me.

Total: _____

Game #14

_____ I feel good about giving to worthy causes.

_____ I feel particularly good about myself when I give.

_____ I sometimes give when I feel pressured to give.

_____ My parents volunteered a lot and encouraged me to do the same.

_____ I give when I have more than enough.

_____ I give sometimes when I don't have much to share but want to give anyway.

_____ I have given or volunteered anonymously.

_____ I tithe some portion of my income each year to organizations or churches of my choice.

_____ I confess I sometimes give because I feel guilty.

_____ I began giving and volunteering after a life crisis.

Total: _____

Game #15

_____ I am living a balanced life with my money and my time.

_____ I have pared down my lifestyle and gotten rid of things, preoccupations, and interests that were just costing me time and money.

_____ I live a socially responsible life that includes being aware of the impact of my actions on others.

_____ I don't deprive myself of the things I need but I don't hoard either.

_____ I give of my resources and myself, both using my name and anonymously.

_____ I have shed a lot of the stress in my life by cutting down on food, alcohol, obsessions, and pastimes that weren't good for me.

_____ I have gotten rid of most of my debt.

_____ I have learned to live off more of my assets rather than struggling to climb over my liabilities.

_____ I have taken charge of my money life and make my own financial decisions.

_____ I know exactly where I am financially from week to week.

Total: _____

Scoring

Record your total check marks for each game below, then note the games in which you scored five or more. Here are the names of the games that were assessed above, along with the numbers of the chapters where you'll learn more about them.

Game #1:   **The More Money Game**. . . . . Chapter Three
Game #2:   **The Victim Game** . . . . Chapter Four
Game #3:   **The Money and Sex Game** . . Chapter Five
Game #4:   **The Workaholic Game**. . . . . . Chapter Six
Game #5:   **The Bag Lady Game** . . . . Chapter Seven
Game #6:   **The Got-More Game** . . . . Chapter Eight
Game #7:   **The Old Money Game**. . . . . . Chapter Nine
Game #8:   **The Social Climber Game** . . . Chapter Ten
Game #9:   **The Self-Worth Game** . . . . . . Chapter Eleven
Game #10: **The Kiddo Game**. . . . . Chapter Twelve
Game #11: **The Mistrust Game** . . . . Chapter Thirteen
Game #12: **The Moneyholic Game** . . . . . Chapter Fourteen
Game #13: **The Slave Game** . . . . Chapter Fifteen
Game #14: **The Giving Game** . . . . Chapter Sixteen
Game #15: **The Simplify Game**. . . . . Chapter Seventeen

Part II

What We Play

Chapter Three

Game #1: The More Money Game

Bob's Story

Bob was fifty-two when I met him. He'd just sold his second start-up company in ten years and made $5 million free and clear after taxes. He said he really enjoyed making money and that "more was better." However, he was now interested in letting his money work for him.

Bob, claiming he was tired of the hustle and bustle, said he wanted to "take it easy." So he invested $2 million in municipal bonds, which were paying a tax-free 8 percent then. Bob figured he could live on that interest, plus an additional income stream from a $3 million investment in apartments.

Within a year, though, Bob grew impatient. He said he needed more money to be happy and live life as he wanted. Bob told me he had decided to sell his apartments, take the proceeds, and place them into a collectible item that he thought he could sell later for double. With the rest of his money he wanted to buy stock in his neighbor's company, a technology start-up.

Bob and I discussed exactly how much income would be required to satisfy his needs. He said that he wasn't sure, but he just

45

knew inside that what he had coming in now wasn't enough. This was my first inkling that Bob had a money demon that was creating his irrational behavior.

I asked Bob if he knew any inside information about his neighbor's firm. If he did, I told him, it wouldn't be legal to invest in that company. Bob said he had heard a few things, but his neighbor would never tell him anything that wasn't public information. We then went on to discuss the downside of investing in just that one stock. Bob finally agreed to limit his investment to 10,000 shares of this start-up.

Sadly, the stock dropped from 50 to 10 in a few short months. Soon I learned that Bob, without telling me, had purchased another $1 million of this same stock at another brokerage. Bob tried to persuade me to let him sell his municipal bonds to purchase even more of the technology stock. I wouldn't do it; I felt it wasn't prudent.

Bob continued to complain that he couldn't live on what he had, even though this was more income than he'd ever had. Bob had a significant need for ego status with his money that translated into *more, more, more.* Unknown to me, Bob was also operating under an even more insidious safety need. Apparently, his father and his grandfather had both lost all of their money. On some deep, unconscious level, he feared the same would happen to him, so he took big risks to counter the fear. Bob transferred his account when I wouldn't agree with his buying more of this tech stock.

A few years later I had lunch with Bob. He told me how he had lost almost everything. The technology company went bankrupt, and he lost nearly all of his investment. Bob and his wife, Carol, were now living in a small condo that had once been their initial investment property. Later, he had taken a job as a chief financial officer in a small company. He was now living a modest life, enjoying his time with his grandchildren.

He described himself as "thankful" that he could stop his destructive need for money. "I saw that having more money only made me more obsessed. I'm glad I could stop the cycle of destructive money before I passed it on to my children." He added, "You know, when I had what seemed like everything in the world materially, I was miserable. Now, with a modest lifestyle, I'm the happiest I've ever been." Bob then apologized for the desperation he had shown when he demanded that his municipal bond portfolio be liquidated. He had felt as if he might as well roll the dice one more time. "After all, I had pulled it off twice before. Why couldn't I do it one more time?"

We momentarily glanced into each other's eyes. I think he realized, as I did, that if he had been successful that last time, Bob would have continued to up the ante until he failed, allowing him to break his pact with his current Money Game. Bob had consciously known that there were healthier ways to end the game. But he'd been unwilling to walk down those paths. "I just couldn't get past the black cloud I inherited from my father and grandfather. They were pretty negative about money, and I guess I took this way to deal with it."

In parting, Bob said he had a lot to be thankful for: He still had his wife, who had stuck by him throughout the unraveling of this Money Game, and he was alive and at peace working on improving his money consciousness. $

The More Money Game: Never Enough

The More Money Game works on the illusion that if we have more money, we'll be on easy street. We won't have to go to work, stress over bills, or be concerned with what we need to save. There will be no future worries. We can watch sports, pursue our hobbies, and travel with our partners.

The Belief

Many people, particularly men, have become accustomed to a low-frequency noise in their minds that nags them about their money problems. For many, it's a constant chatter that goes something like this: "It sure would be nice if we could build a pool for the kids" or

"If I could just make enough money to take Sally to Bermuda, I think she would fall for me." This mental noise is like background music. Some people get so used to it that it's like a low-grade fever that they don't even know is reverberating in their heads.

The problem with this game is that it's insatiable. It places happiness outside ourselves in the form of money. We put our peace of mind in money to shore up our fears. The drawback to this kind of belief system is that we become a bottomless pit. Sometimes—as with the folks at Enron or WorldCom—in order to meet this insatiable need, we have to bend the rules more and more to get the money to fill up that pit. The problem is that every time we fill up, we're hungry later. Soon there's a major price to pay for this expended energy. Getting more money becomes an addiction, and we are hooked.

The Secret

The secret of this game is the worry within ourselves. High ego needs suggest ego fragility. When we put our faith in money as our savior instead of in ourselves, we are living on quicksand. It's a scary place to be because it's so shaming. We may resort to anything to avoid being exposed: more risk taking, gambling, greed, coercion, and larceny. We escalate the risks in hopes of once and for all slaying the dragon within us, so we can walk away from the driving obsession that seems to have taken control of our lives.

Game Triggers

Age and life events are key triggers for the More Money Game. By the time we are adults, we have often internalized some kind of "money timeline" in our heads. This timeline tells us we should be at a certain point in terms of money accumulation. For example, if your father was a millionaire at thirty-five, and you are thirty-four and competitive with your father, chances are you'll start to panic and your More Money Game dynamic will kick in. In another case, your parents may have died at age forty-two and you may fear a similar fate. Your More Money Game may take the form of a desperate lunge in your late thirties to achieve prosperity.

The key to understanding these triggers is to explore how many "shoulds" lurk in your money consciousness. Look hard at your beliefs, find the list of "shoulds," and you'll find the source of your anxiety. Some typical money "shoulds" include:

- I should have at least a year's worth of salary in the bank by age thirty.
- I should own my own home by now.
- I should be debt-free by age thirty-five; if I'm not debt-free by that age, I'll never make it.
- I should be making $100,000 a year by now. After all, I'm forty.
- I have three kids heading to college in the next five years. I should have $50,000 set aside for tuition by now.
- My cousins on both sides of the family own two or more houses. I should own that many homes, but I am struggling to pay one mortgage right now.
- All my close friends from college drive Mercedes-Benz or Lexus cars. I'm still in a Toyota. I should be doing better than this.

Sometimes a More Money Game dynamic may lie dormant in your unconscious for years and then be triggered by some life event, such as:

- A daughter or son's wedding
- A close colleague or friend's getting a large raise
- Being passed over for a promotion
- For the first time, your spouse makes more money than you
- A heart attack, stroke, or brush with a major disease
- Your partner's sudden decision to leave you
- Your turning a particularly emotion-triggering age like thirty-five, forty, fifty, or sixty

Disarming Strategies

Once these More Money Game triggers kick in, there are still ways to disengage yourself from the process. To do so, however, you will need to ask yourself some tough questions and really prioritize what you want in life. Some ways to disengage include the following:

> Ask yourself if getting more money right now is something *you* want or if you are fulfilling someone else's dream, like a father's, mother's, partner's, or uncle's.
>
> Take stock of where you are right now in your life. Find a quiet place where you won't be disturbed, then fold a piece of paper in half vertically and make two columns: "Where I Am in My Life" and "Where I Think I Should Be in My Life." List your answers, then read them aloud. Put a check mark by the things that are really important to your self-satisfaction and not just to your need to be valued by others. Notice what you might be able to live without.
>
> Take a series of index cards and write one money "should" on each. This is something you believe you should accomplish with your resources and life goals. Read the cards through and put them in three piles: "Will Do," "Should Do," "Not Sure." Then look through all three stacks, read them out loud, and pull out the ones your gut tells you that you really have an aversion to doing. These are the reject cards. Tear these cards up, then (a) throw them away, (b) burn them, or (c) flush them down the toilet. They don't belong in your life and are only dragging you down. Once you have your remaining cards, proceed to the section titled, "Your Action Plan," below.

Your New Way of Thinking

"I will get real with myself. I'll admit my fear and take back my life. I'll begin to manage my money from a position of strength, not dependency, and I'll separate my ego from my stuff. I'll hold the tension within me as I explore my inner fears and bring myself back into alignment with my higher self and purpose."

Your Action Plan

Inner steps to take:

1. Take fifteen large sticky notes and write your top life priorities, using one idea per note. Include your money priorities. Post the priorities on a wall, step back, and look at them as a group. Next, tear up the one you can live without. Review your remaining priorities. Then tear them up until you have only five. Notice what you have left. Take a hard look at whether you really want these in your life.

2. Write a paragraph about who you are *without* your money. If it's a short paragraph, get to work expanding yourself as a balanced human being and broaden your interests.

3. Try relating to people instead of to money. Try to create at least one new relationship that doesn't involve money.

4. Avoid beating yourself up and taking the polar-opposite stance toward money. Don't give up all your money in order to become a "money saint." Such an action would still be your ego at work.

5. Allow for periods of uncertainty with money as you formulate a new belief system.

6. Find a new money mantra. Say instead, "I use money with discretion. I am in control, and I am content."

7. Make a list of the ten most important events of your life. Then reflect on them: How many involved money? Do you want more of the nonmoney ones? How can you get them?

Financial steps to take:

1. Give some money anonymously. Discover the experience of giving your money without being known for it or expecting something in return.

2. Take your "Will Do" cards from the "Disarming Strategies" section above and create a reasonable timeline for your money goals and actions you really want to take, for yourself, not for someone else.

3. One day a month, resolve not to use money at all. Buy nothing. Carry no cash, write no checks, keep your credit card at home. Experience what it's like to be a nonconsumer.

4. Seek pursuits where money won't help you: Go rock climbing or hiking, build trails in the woods, plant trees in the city, try your hand at painting or sculpture, learn to play the piano or the guitar.

5. Seek meaning in nonfinancial relationships: Volunteer at a soup kitchen, become a mentor to a young person, join Habitat for Humanity, become part of a book group, or join a literacy program.

Think about It

"Money never made a man happy yet, nor will it. There is nothing in its nature to produce happiness. The more a man has, the more he wants. Instead of filling a vacuum, it makes one."

—Benjamin Franklin

THE MORE MONEY GAME	
Rules	Get as much as you can because money alleviates worry.
Belief	If I have more money, I'll be happier.
Secret	People don't know how much I worry.
Feeling	Chronic worry, fear, emptiness
Game Triggers	Age, life events, death, illness, divorce, separation, marriage, children leaving for college or getting married
Disarming Strategies	Get rid of "shoulds"; create a realistic money timeline for your money goals.
Persona	Hungry Ghost
Action	Take charge of what you really want.

Chapter Four

Game #2: The Victim Game

Linda's Story

Linda is a top sales executive in a pharmaceuticals company. She has no formal sales training and only an associate's business degree from a local college, but she is a stellar sales representative. She not only fights hard to make her sales quota each month, but she puts in an extra ten or twenty hours a week so she can earn quarterly top sales awards.

When Linda wins these awards, she celebrates with her husband, Gavin, and promptly hands him her bonus. Gavin controls all the money in the family. He pays the bills, manages all their assets, and watches their investment portfolio. Linda has no idea where the money goes. She often says, "Gavin has the brains in our marriage. I'm so lucky to have him."

Gavin owns a modest restaurant business. He enjoys lounging at his restaurant late into the night with his favorite customers. He's been known to have an affair or two, although Linda seems oblivious to this. He makes only about 40 percent of what Linda makes, but he never tells her that. Instead, he buys her a piece of jewelry here, a weekend vacation there, and she thinks he makes most of the money.

Here's how Gavin controls Linda's knowledge of their finances: She carries her own checkbook, and every few weeks Gavin deposits some money into that account. However, when Linda writes checks, she never deducts the amounts. Every week or so, Linda hands over the checkbook so he can balance it for her. Gavin allows Linda to have two credit cards. When the bills come in, Gavin pays them. Sometimes Linda severely overspends, and Gavin becomes irate.

When they were first married, Gavin made a couple of inkpad stamps so he could send Linda messages about her spending. One has a happy face on it; the other, an unhappy face. When Linda keeps her credit-card spending in check, Gavin briefly shows her that month's bills marked with a happy face. When Linda overspends, she's shown a stack of bills with an unhappy face on top. At those times, Linda laughs and says she feels "terribly bad about how I can't control my money. Thank heaven for Gavin. He knows how to handle things." $

The Victim Game: Surrendering Control

This is a common game when we feel we aren't competent to make or manage our own money. We play this game by depending on others to make most of the money or control the money in the relationship. This can happen to either men or women, although women seem to fall victim to a greater degree.

This involves failing to take responsibility. Women and men both play this game by turning over money to spouses or financial advisors with carte blanche to manage it as they see fit. Women surrender this power fairly easily because it has typically been assumed that men know more about managing finances. Until 1970, women weren't permitted to have credit cards in most cases, except in their husband's or father's name. So they have had only thirty years or so to catch up to the money savvy that many men have or are assumed to have. The flip side is that men are expected to act like they know a lot about money even though they may have been taught nothing about it. As psychotherapist and author Olivia Mellan points out, men generally are trained to mask their areas of incompetence and assume an air of authority, especially around money, whether justified or not.

The Victim Game is typically an "I'm smart and you're not" game that involves two roles: a manipulator and a controller. The controller and manipulator play a one-up/one-down game, with the manipulator (Linda in the above example) typically taking the one-down position on a conscious level. On an unconscious level, the roles may, in fact, be reversed. The controller (Gavin) may be constantly in the one-down, catch-up position because the manipulator uses indirect coercion or "money accidents" to get what he or she wants.

In both cases, a lack of money awareness exists. Neither party is willing to draw boundaries that force each party to be responsible for his or her own financial consciousness. Anytime we step in and take on a financial task for another, we are doing a disservice to both the other person and to ourselves. We are depriving that person of learning how to live a balanced financial life and are making him or her dependent on us. Ideally, we should choose to come neither from strength nor weakness with money, but instead to become financially integrated individuals.

The Belief

A deep belief in incompetence underlies this game. There is a feeling that "I'm not good enough, and when it comes to money, I am hopelessly out of my league. So I will manipulate and play the poor-me role to get what I want." On the flip side, the other partner takes the "I know more than you" role so he (or she) can dominate in order to feel better about himself.

Linda is typical of those who avoid money in general and/or let a stronger partner take charge of the finances. Sometimes this happens in couples in order to keep peace in the family. More often, individuals, typically women, will marry for money and financial support.

Controllers like Gavin relish the "I'm smarter" role and often find a partner (or teach their children) to play the "lesser" role. From a needs-hierarchy perspective, the controller has high esteem and belonging needs, whereas the manipulator has high safety and belonging needs. Both need each other and maneuver between up and down positions and back again.

Neither role is healthy because each lacks clarity and respect. Just as in sports where athletes play multiple positions and can substitute for one another, both partners need to be versatile by becoming money aware. The ideal premise is for a couple to be comfortable enough in their relationship to take turns paying the bills, managing the assets, and doing the budget.

The Secret

The secret of the Victim Game is an underlying disrespect and, sometimes, resentment toward the other player. This is, in fact, not an "I love you, let me take care of you" game. It is a "You are so pathetic, I can control or manipulate everything you do" game.

The Victim Game is indirect. Needs are unspoken. There's a desperate need to cover up vulnerabilities. Sometimes the game escalates into a vicious hide-and-seek with money and assets. The roles become easily reversed because neither partner trusts the other to be direct with his or her thoughts and feelings. It becomes a game of collusion. Each must be rescued or outmaneuvered. This often occurs in families when strong emotional bonds compete with desperate safety and control money needs. An ugly tennis match ensues, with each player trying to buy or repel the other's love.

Unfortunately, this is a corrosive game. It keeps both players in a corner, away from their real needs for money understanding and compassion. Money becomes a currency whereby love is given or withheld. The outcome of this game is rarely gratitude, because there are so many strings attached. The more likely outcome is resentment, anger, and even loathing.

Game Triggers

This game is typically triggered by a money relationship, whether between spouses or partners, parents and children, siblings, or other relatives (like cousins). Women often enter this game when they are forced to deal with complex money dealings like buying a house, making major investments or purchases, getting married, having children, or inheriting money.

Likewise, men may move into either role once they're in a money relationship in which they feel insecure or uncertain how to behave. They may feel forced to fall back on learned patterns of behavior. Men whose fathers, for instance, controlled every aspect of the family finances may suddenly become money tyrants once they're married or in a relationship.

Sometimes a couple (or even an individual) will move into the victim dynamic in the presence of a new, strong financial advisor. They may feel compelled to surrender all their financial dealings to the financial expert, warranted or not. The same may be true when lawyers become involved in trusts, probate, or real estate dealings.

Often the death of a close relative who seriously impacted the victim or controller's early money education will trigger Victim Game behaviors. For example, the death of a rich uncle who leaves all his money to a nephew instead of a son may trigger the victim/controller dynamic, casting the son as the victim and the nephew in the role of controller. Likewise, when dying parents leave wills favoring one child over another, the Victim/controller Game might begin in earnest between siblings at that time (if not before).

Disarming Strategies

One of the key strategies for disengaging from the Victim Game is gaining money knowledge. Taking a class and learning about wills, trusts, real estate, and other investments can make individuals more confident in money matters. Admitting your lack of experience, and then taking action, can build self-esteem.

Other strategies that can lessen or avert Victim/controller Money Games include talking candidly about money issues, being assertive, and asking questions. Be honest with yourself about your motivations. If you are keeping money secrets, ask yourself, "What is the benefit to me of being secretive?" Then, explore if it's worth it to you to manipulate to get what you want.

Further, ask yourself, "What else do I need to do to feel good about how I deal with money with my partner, spouse, child, father, mother, etc.?" Then ask yourself, "How can I take responsibility for feeling good about how I operate in my life with money?"

Your New Way of Thinking

"I am competent with my money. I can learn what I need to know and take ownership of my money actions. I respect myself first and am honest with my needs both to myself and to others. I take charge of my money and my life. I respect others and expect them to take charge of their own money and lives. We live on an equal footing. We share joint responsibility with shared money."

Your Action Plan

Inner steps to take:

1. Recognize the signs of hidden money safety issues. Do you get a sinking feeling when you need to balance your checkbook, talk to money people, or do anything with investments? Do you wake up with nightmares about money handling? Do you regularly hand over your money management to someone else? Draw up a list of your worst fears, then write a sentence or two about what you would do in the worst-case scenario. Use that plan in an emergency or to calm yourself when you feel anxious about your money.

2. Work with a therapist to open lines of communication and seek a role reversal. Note that when either partner controls all the money, imbalance results. No one person or group knows *everything* about anything. If you're the "victim," work hard at empowering yourself and assuming more control. If you're the controller, encourage yourself to let go and allow your partner a greater voice. That will lead to a healthier relationship.

3. Explore your money past to determine if fear and incompetence is a learned family and societal role for you. As a first step, use the Money History Assessment at the end of this chapter.

4. Sit down with your partner and discuss money values, beliefs, money accounts and actions, and money plans. Even twenty years or more into a marriage is not too late. Be open and honest about what you believe, what you have, and where the two of you should be headed.

Financial steps to take:

If you're in the "victim" role:

1. Rank your money knowledge in the following areas on a scale of 1 to 10 (with 10 being highly comfortable with your knowledge):

   ____   Checking account maintenance

   ____   Savings account maintenance

   ____   Debt payment and scheduling

   ____   Budgeting

   ____   Real estate investment

   ____   Basic investment (money-market accounts, CDs, etc.)

   ____   Basic financial planning

   ____   Mid-level investment (stocks, bonds, etc.)

   ____   Basic retirement planning

   ____   High-level investment (futures, options, commodities, etc.)

   ____   Commercial investment

2. Educate yourself on your weakest areas as revealed above. Take a course in money management, perhaps at a community college, to gain an understanding of the basics.

3. Create a budget. Start by keeping a log of all dollars spent for three months. Then break that down into categories so you can see where the money is going.

4. If big debts are an issue, join Debtors Anonymous; consult with a debt-consolidating organization or even a bankruptcy attorney.

5. Establish a relationship with a financial counselor, whether a CPA, a financial planner, or some other professional. Get from the counselor an overall assessment on how you're doing with money and what you need to do next.

6. Begin to slowly assert yourself in the management of your own and the joint financial affairs. For example, this year master the checkbook and paying bills. Make next year the one in which you pay off all nonmortgage debts. The following year, seek to become fully informed about your individual/joint investments. After that, tackle the retirement accounts.

If you're in the controlling role:

1. Help educate your partner about your joint financial affairs. Be patient and keep in mind that you're trying to help undo years of conditioning. So, carefully explain what you're doing with money and why.

2. Fully disclose all assets and share that information.

3. Begin to cede exclusive control. First, share the checkbook, then the debts and the investments, and finally the retirement accounts. Make these joint territories, not individual fiefdoms.

Think about It

"Love of money often makes a man a coward, but love of power always makes a man a brute. It is the most degrading love of all. Love of material well-being seldom hurts others, but love of power and glory always does."

—Lin Yutang

THE VICTIM GAME	
Rules	I'm incompetent with money matters. I can't take care of myself, so I will find someone who will.
Belief	I am not capable on my own. If I fend for myself, it won't be enough.
Secret	I love you for what you do for me, but deep down I resent the hell out of you for making me dependent.
Feeling	Indirect anger, incompetence
Game Triggers	New relationships, old relationships, children being born, getting divorced or married, relatives dying, inheriting money, losing major amounts of money, losing a job
Disarming Strategies	Learn everything you need to know about money so you will feel comfortable taking responsibility for your actions. Disengage from manipulation. Talk openly about your fears, concerns, issues, hopes, and desires.
Persona	Leech
Action	Take charge.

Money History Assessment

For the ages indicated, list any money memories you have, what lessons you think you learned, and who taught them to you.

Examples:

Ages 1 to 5 Years

Memory: I have a memory of my father giving me four shiny quarters and telling me to save two and spend two. He said, "Always save half for your piggy bank first, then spend the rest elsewhere."

Lessons Learned: I think my father was trying to give me the idea to save before I spend. He always believed in this until the day he died.

Who Taught Me: My father

Ages 6 to 10 Years

Memory: I remember once trying to steal some bubble gum from the local five-and-dime. My mother caught me and made me take it back to the manager and apologize. I didn't get dessert for a week.

Lessons Learned: I learned that stealing didn't pay. Now I get a stomachache if ever I think about taking anything, even a paper clip.

Who Taught Me: My mother

Your own history:

Ages 1 to 5 Years

Memory: _____

_____

_____

Lessons Learned: _____

_____

_____

Who Taught Me: _____

Ages 6 to 10 Years

Memory: _____

_____

_____

Lessons Learned: _____

_____

_____

Who Taught Me: _____

Ages 11 to 15 Years

Memory: _____

_____

_____

Lessons Learned: _____

_____

_____

Who Taught Me: _____

Ages 16 to 20 Years

Memory: _____

_____

_____

Lessons Learned: _____

_____

_____

Who Taught Me: _____

Ages 21 to 30 Years

Memory: _____

_____

_____

Lessons Learned: _____

_____

_____

Who Taught Me: _____

Ages 31 to 40 Years

Memory: _____

_____

_____

Lessons Learned: _____

_____

_____

Who Taught Me: _____

Ages 41 to 50 Years

Memory: _____

_____

_____

Lessons Learned: _____

_____

_____

Who Taught Me: _____

50 Years and Older

Memory: _____

_____

_____

Lessons Learned: _____

_____

_____

Who Taught Me: _____

What patterns emerge from your money history? (For example, "I notice my family emphasized saving money and I hated that so I have always refused to do it" or "My parents fought about money a lot when I was a teenager, and I saw my mother sneaking money all the time from my dad. I notice now I don't tell my spouse everything about what I am spending.")

_____

_____

_____

_____

How do these patterns of behavior show up in your Money Games now? (For example, "I can't help but hide money from my husband now" or "I suddenly became a saver when my divorce wiped me out.")

_____

_____

_____

_____

Chapter Five

Game #3: The Money and Sex Game

William's Story

William is a successful airline pilot now in his mid-to-late forties. When I first met William and his wife, Nancy, they were in their late twenties and seeking financial advice. Early in his career, William would take on extra flight assignments to get ahead financially. He found himself out of the country on international flights nearly three weeks each month. Initially, this was fine with both William and his wife. Nancy was busy raising four young children and liked the extra money William would earn.

They had been married right out of high school, and William was a military pilot for seven years. He then jumped to the airlines. To justify his time away from the family as a commercial pilot, William would always buy lavish presents for the kids and his wife and take them on great vacations to places like Bali, Alaska, and Italy.

The trouble began when the children started growing up and Nancy had time for herself. Wanting more of William's time, Nancy grew bored. She ventured out of the marriage and found a dot-com man who had both more money and more time to spend with her.

William was shattered. He thought he made plenty of money and had an exciting, sexy career. He thought that because he made lots of money, Nancy would always be attracted to him and love him. He had lived the myth of a high-earning, high-flying pilot and thought his wife had bought into the relationship completely. Unfortunately, his belief blew up in his face. He grew gravely depressed.

Nancy was reportedly "happier than I've ever been" for a while, but the bottom fell out when the dot-com man's company went belly-up. She divorced him and moved on to an even richer man.

William reassessed his priorities after a long, hard look at his life. He decided to live a much simpler life. He cut back on his flying time, rejecting any extra flight assignments. He spent more time with his children. William also did some soul searching and found there was more than his money and career that made him attractive. He developed his talents as golfer, took some courses in art, learned how to paint, and began to put his pilot persona into perspective with who he was as an individual.

Ultimately, he found a woman to share his life with who put little store in his value as a pilot and wanted him because he was a loving, caring companion. They share interests in golfing, painting, and long walks each morning on the beach with their dog. They are now planning for a scaled-down retirement. $

The Money and Sex Game: Quid Pro Quo

Also known as the quid pro quo syndrome, this game is frequently played out in male-female relationships, although it is evident in some gay and lesbian couples as well. Many of us are acculturated to believe that the best way we can attract a partner is to show off our earning and sex prowess as a breadwinner. Our sex appeal becomes entwined with our earning power and our ability to "score" success. Our "scoring" acumen is based more on our flash than on who we are as individuals.

The Money and Sex Game is a superficial one that many of us learn to play as a result of societal pressures. It's a game based on appearances, and it's difficult to escape because our American society is steeped in it. Even if we ourselves have a rich depth of feeling and connectedness, we often have to submerge these aspects of ourselves under a more popular public image.

Classic egotists, the participants in this game are essentially playing a narcissistic self-esteem game with themselves and their partners. Typically, the arrangement between colluding partners mandates a lifelong commitment based on money for sex and sex for money (that's the quid pro quo). One partner says, "I will earn money and status and you will love me for it." The other partner responds, "I will adore you, give you sex, and stay attractive to keep up my part of the deal."

The deal is often based primarily on what the players have and can deliver, and not as much on who they are. As such, the players themselves can be easily interchanged. The faces can change as long as the dynamic feels the same. Couples who can get past the superficiality of these agreements (often after some life crisis) can find rich relationships. When they can't get past the superficiality, they sometimes simply "upgrade" to new partners.

The Belief

Men and women approach this game somewhat differently. For men, there is a deep-seated ego belief system around earning an income and having an attractive career. Because men are typically breadwinners, this drive makes some sense. But too often it becomes an obsession to the exclusion of any other personality development.

For women, there is an equally strong belief in a woman's need to relate to others, whether this is in the field of commerce or romance. Women can be primary breadwinners as well, of course, but often feel compelled to twist themselves into the "superwoman persona" if they have chosen the breadwinner route. They may re-create themselves into paragons of athleticism, attractiveness (through implants, face lifts, etc.), intelligence, and money prowess. If they choose the subordinate role, they may feel pressured to maintain a beautiful body and physical sexiness in order to deliver the counterpart to their partner's earning prowess.

Whether superman or superwoman, each will usually seek a mate who not only reflects that burnished image, but enhances it. Typically those mates will be similar in types; that is, narcissism will meet narcissism (rich man/attractive woman or rich woman/attractive man), and so the quid pro quo will occur.

In a world where we are constantly measured and weighed by appearances, we can't ignore the rules of mating in our society. I have worked with several late-thirtysomething career women who prove this game is being played by women as well as men. These women are in burgeoning careers. Many have successfully managed their money and are now looking for husbands to start families. They tell me, "I want a 'player'—he has to be attractive, virile, and doesn't have to make too much money since I make a lot. I don't want an old one, or an ugly one. Frankly, I've earned this kind of man."

On the flip side, many men look for mates who will be awed by their prowess but still remain subordinate and provide a certain image and fertility when it comes to having a family. Sociologists have found that men have a primordial instinct to seek healthy, attractive, amenable women (health and youth are keys) because they must be fertile child bearers. Alternatively, the typical non-breadwinner female looks most for a productive male breadwinner and, hence, an older man with earning power may win her affections over a younger, more attractive man who lacks earning acumen.

As long as the players maintain their prescribed roles and "keep up appearances," the quid pro quo remains intact over the life of the relationship. It is when a better earner appears, or a face begins to sag, or the attraction lessens, that the game wanes. Sadly, it may end in a whimper.

The Secret

The secret of the Money and Sex Game is the belief that we need to give something to get something. The Money and Sex Game player's mantra is: "What can you do for me?" As long as we deliver, whether it's money or sex or children or adoration or mutual funds or Harry Winston diamonds, we are safe. But Money and Sex Game players have a hard time shaking an inner whisper that constantly asks, "Am I enough?"

Some Money and Sex Game players experience the effects of this game as low-grade paranoia. They don't trust their mates because they don't trust themselves. To simply be who they are would be to expose themselves without armor. This game is rooted in a secret, deep-seated belief that stems from insecurity. Players fear they won't be wanted for who they are, only for what they have to offer. And if they lose their attractiveness in some way, they will lose the love of their mates (and other potential mates) as well.

Game Triggers

Usually, we start playing or rejecting this game as early as our pre-teen years. Triggers for this game often appear hand in hand with sexual tension. For example, we begin to notice certain girls/women are attracted to men who dress a certain way, drive a certain car, live a certain lifestyle. We notice certain boys/men date and marry women who have certain looks, have certain jobs and education, have a certain orientation to life. We discover quickly that these attractors may or may not require money (for clothes, cars, education, drugs, athletic prowess, sports, bank accounts, vacations, and so on), and the game begins.

Our parents' interactions and those of close peers will often set the tone for how our sexuality gets magnified or diminished by money. If we become dependent on stuff to make us attractive, the dependency becomes a voracious need for more and more goods, appearances, or accomplishments to keep us desirable.

There are many triggers for this dynamic over the course of a lifetime. Any of the following will propel us into some stage of panic if we have bought into this myth:

- We get fired.
- We lose a house, car, company, title.
- Our skin starts to sag or we start to go gray.
- We approach middle age and/or menopause.
- We haven't had children and are approaching middle age.
- We become parents.
- We become grandparents.
- A younger person shows sexual interest in us.
- Our spouse or mate leaves us for someone we perceive is richer, sexier, better looking, younger, or smarter.
- A close friend starts a new company.
- We change careers.
- We go back to school.

Disarming Strategies

Disengaging from the Money and Sex Game triggers can take time. Probably because our culture puts such value on looks and possessions, our self-perception focuses for much of our lives on what we have or how we look. However, a life change or crisis like death, illness, sagging skin, or money problems will often force us to take a hard look at who we are. The stuff is abandoning us. We are being forced to evaluate how naked we are as people, to reassess how much our self-worth is a reflection of someone else's opinion.

One disarming strategy is to simply take a deep breath. Focus on your breath and reassure yourself that you can handle anything that follows. Then gently ask yourself the following questions:

- Am I my face?
- Am I my money?
- Am I my house?
- Am I my car?
- Am I my portfolio?
- Am I my body?

Remind yourself of your coping skills. If you didn't already have such skills and a handle on who you are, you wouldn't be reading this book and seeking answers. Now reinforce those coping skills. Draft a "How I Coped" timeline. Take a large piece of paper (or tape several 8" × 11" sheets end-to-end) and draw a line an inch or two from the long edge of the paper (or papers). Number the line in five-inch segments, starting with number 1. Your line will look something like this:

1	5	10	15	20	25	etc.

These numbers represent your ages in increments of five. Beneath the line at the age points, make a list of the ways that you coped with relationships, life changes, changes in your body, and how you handled rejections or acceptances. You will probably find that you have a lot of skills for dealing with life changes and relationships, including your ability to attract others through money, looks, stuff, or education, as well as your savvy, compassion, capacity to overcome fear, commitment, and more.

Finally, ask yourself this difficult question: *Is this relationship or arrangement worth what I am having to do or be to keep it?* Then, on a scale of 1 to 10 (with 1 being "I am good enough in this relationship just as I am" and 10 being "I am afraid I will never have, be, earn enough to keep this relationship"), rate yourself on how comfortable you are with the arrangement. If you score above a 5, consider what you need to do to disengage from the game or come clean with your partner about your fears.

Your New Way of Thinking

"I will define my success based on who I am, my intentions, and my authentic actions in life."

Your Action Plan

Inner steps to take:

1. Fold a piece of paper in half vertically and create two lists of your qualities: "What I Offer" and "What I Am." In the "What I Offer" column, list your stuff (bank accounts, houses, cars, and so on). In the "What I Am" column, list your personal traits (such as loving, skilled, focused, committed, goal-directed, compassionate). Now asterisk the items in both lists that you emphasize most in your relationships. Consider how much of "What I Am" you are sharing in your relationships.

2. Now try this: Take another piece of paper, fold it in half vertically, and create lists of two other qualities: "What I Think My Mate (or Previous Mates) Thinks I Offer" and "What My Mate(s) Thinks I Am." In the first column, list the stuff (bank accounts, houses, cars, and so on) for which you think your mate values you. In the second column, list your personal traits (loving, skilled, focused, committed, goal-directed, compassionate) for which you think your mate values you. Then asterisk the items in either list that you think he or she puts the most emphasis on in your relationship. Compare your two sets of lists and consider how real your relationships are and how you want them to be in the future.

3. Beware of going to the opposite extreme of masking what you have and hiding or lying about your assets. This sets in motion a different Money Game and can be equally destructive. Balance truth with prudence in using money in relationships.

Financial steps to take:

If you're in the "male" (big-spending) role:

1. Add up the cost in hard numbers of what it took to land your recent mate or keep the one you have. Take into account purchases made preparatory to or during the

romance. Did you buy a car in part for its sexual allure? A nicer house or apartment? Jewelry? Clothes? Vacations you otherwise wouldn't have taken?

Is the total more than $10,000? More than $100,000? Greater than $250,000? The higher the total, the more stress you are putting on yourself about how much money you have to earn or spend to be loved.

Resolve, first, to rein in these expenses and, second, acknowledge this pattern with your partner. Begin a dialogue about the role of money in the relationship, and at some point, ask him or her point-blank: *Do you love me for who I am or what I own?*

2. Find a low-cost hobby—such as gardening, chess, or hiking—and pursue it for a year as a means of meeting people who have similar interests rather than a connection via money.

3. Rent or borrow an older car, drive it for a month or two, and see if people treat you differently.

If you're the "female" (receiving) role:

1. Investigate how your partner is spending his/your/joint money. Start by asking. If he's not forthcoming, do some investigation on your own. Take a look at the bills, bank statements, tax returns, and brokerage statements.

2. Take responsibility for your financial self-sufficiency. Start by paying off any of your debts. Take a financial education course. Read some books on the subject. Open a savings account. Start and/or manage your retirement accounts.

3. Contact a career counselor, take vocational aptitude tests, and design a career path that has the potential to be exciting and fulfilling.

Think about It

"To be clever enough to get all that money, one must be stupid enough to want it."

—G.K. Chesterton

THE MONEY AND SEX GAME	
Rules	Money gets me sex and love, so I need to show I make a lot of it to be loved.
Belief	My money makes me more attractive than I would be without it.
Secret	No one would want me without my money.
Feeling	Worthless, lonely, not enough
Game Triggers	Life changes (empty nesting, menopause, retirement), changes in body (hair, skin, athleticism), changes in financial status or earning power, divorce, spousal death
Disarming Strategies	Focus on who you are rather than what you have or look like, assess the degree of game playing (manipulations) you are doing to get or keep a relationship, get centered and get real about who you are with others.
Persona	Sexless Sam
Action	Be who you are, not your looks or your stuff.

Money and Sex Assessment

After the following statements, write *T* for those that are true for you, and *F* for those that are false.

1. I have used my financial assets to get attention from others. ____

2. I have used my physical attractiveness to get attention from those who have money. ____

3. I tend to turn over the finances to my partner because I don't want to deal with them. ____

4. I sometimes give sex when my partner gives me something first (presents, vacations, cash, approves a decision I've made, yields on an issue, agrees to do something I've asked him/her to do, etc.). ____

5. I buy my loved ones gifts and/or take them places to earn and maintain their love. ____

6. I have felt less than desirable when I have lost my job, failed to get a promotion, or been out of work. ____

7. I have used my attractiveness to get jobs or to get ahead in my career. ____

8. As I get older, I have to admit that I rely more on my income, house, cars, and estate to make me attractive to others. ____

9. I sometimes wonder if I am worthy of being loved if I didn't have money. ____

10. I sometimes wonder if others would really want me without my attractiveness. ____

11. I have ongoing conflict with my partner about money. ____

12. I am in a relationship with someone who is really tight with money and I resent him or her for it a little. ____

13. Sometimes I get back at my partner by spending money or running up debts. ____

14. I have secrets about money that I haven't shared with my partner. ____

15. Speaking about money is too difficult, and we, as a couple, avoid it whenever possible. ____

Count up the number of *T*s. If you answered more than six of these questions as true, you may be playing a Money and Sex Game.

Chapter Six

Game #4: The Workaholic Game

Richard's Story

Richard, forty, was a stockbroker who told me several stories about his father, a prominent surgeon in a small Ohio town. Richard recalled that his father wasn't around much when he was growing up, and when he was around, the father had to be careful to divide his time equally among the six children.

As he spoke about this, Richard was upset about not having really known his dad. His father worked so long, as chief of surgery at the local hospital, that young Richard would kind of forget what he looked like. As he told me this, Richard perked up and told me that his father had tried hard to make up for it, though. "Things weren't that bad," he said with a lame smile, because his dad "bought us everything we'd ever want and he was a good provider."

The bright spots were the two-week vacations once each year when the father would take the family to a vacation home up in the mountains several states away. Richard fondly recalled the hikes and fishing they would all do together. Once they returned home, his father would go back to work, "slaving away to pay for all the expensive tastes that he said we had."

One of the other highlights of their family life was tax time in April each year. When his father's taxes were done, the whole family would wait to see how "they" made out. If Richard's father had made more money than the year before, he would buy each family member a gift. They would then go out and celebrate at the nicest restaurant in town, and they would take an even better vacation than the year before.

But what Richard wanted most was for his father to have attended Richard's high school football games. Each year his father would promise he would make it to at least one game. He never did. His dad had promised that, no matter what, he would come to Richard's last game his senior year. At halftime Richard scanned the stands, but once again, his dad was a no-show. Richard never forgave him, even though his father bought him a new car to make up for it.

Richard's mom really raised them, and he'd wished many times that his dad had been a teacher or had some other job where he was around more often. Richard felt deeply neglected, and to this day, he says, his father is distant.

As a result, Richard decided to overcompensate in his own relationship with his children. He wasn't going to let his work prevent him from spending time with his children. That's why he would always leave his office as soon as the stock market closed to go home and coach one of his three kids in their sports. In fact, Richard became so overly involved in his kids' lives that if he could have stepped back and observed himself, he would have seen that he had become the polar opposite of his father.

Richard still tries to recapture through his kids the love he didn't get from his dad. He doesn't have a lot of extra money due to his focusing the majority of his energy on his kids.

What Richard has done is to make the mistake of substituting one game (being a good provider proves your love for your family) for another game (being a good dad means devoting 100 percent of your time to your children). Sad to say, what Richard may experience once his children grow up is that his kids may become more distant as they try to escape his overinvolvement in their lives. **$**

The Workaholic Game: Addicted to Your Office

This game involves people falling into the trap of believing, "If I bring home a big paycheck each week, then my family will love me and I will feel fulfilled." The game rules for the Workaholic Game demand complete attention to the goal. Working late, asking for tougher and tougher assignments in the pursuit of higher pay, forsaking holidays, and playing golf on weekends just to network—all the actions that take us away from our home lives are part of the workaholic dynamic. The game is based on unwritten corporate rules that, to be a team player, you have to be willing to commit beyond the call of duty. This means earning your stripes by demonstrating a willingness to forsake all for the company.

When we play this game, we usually have two forces pulling at us: the desire to perform and a fear of not doing enough. Financial necessity breeds fear and demands more work. More work strains day-to-day effectiveness and relationship success, but nets success in terms of the bottom line. Individuals who excel at this game are often the Type A individuals for whom work becomes both a haven and an addiction. They are safe from fear when working, but the work is an all-consuming mistress and demands total focus. For many workaholics, the only acceptable way out is through death or a major health issue requiring hospital time.

The Belief

Self-image and anxiety control are key beliefs in this game. Being a hardworking provider is a measure of worth for many of us, particularly men. In the 1980s, for example, it became a competition to see how many hours one could work. Forty hours became a mere baseline. Work warriors were clocking fifty, fifty-five, sixty, sixty-five hours a week, with no end in sight. Today, we are still hard at work, trying to offset economic instability and planning for an uncertain future. Even experts on quality of work and diminishing returns argue today over the optimal amount of hours worked before quality is completely sacrificed. But many of us keep working long hours nevertheless.

Work warriors often get lots of flak from family and friends over their work habits. Everyone tells them, "You work too much. We never see you." Some work warriors are driven by fear of failure, some by pure money greed. Others are driven by the demands of family and spouses, and yet others by a chronic need to find ego reinforcement in work. All are signs of overdependence on the work ethic.

Work warriors may offset the flak, however, by giving lavish gifts, vacations, or donating large sums to charity. They may justify their long hours at work because it's "for the good of the family," and then bring home presents for family members.

The work itself becomes the second player in the game. The game becomes an ever-expanding playing field since the goalposts move continuously and the game never ends. The workaholic justifies his work by feeling proud when he can buy his family the finest things money can offer as he or she buries guilt in the presents purchased. We play the Workaholic Game in order to get respect and feel safe.

The problem is we never get enough respect. And we never feel safe enough. We look outside for validation. The game essentially plays us. The workaholic is always looking over his shoulder for the enemy—anybody who might try to outperform him and steal the campaign ribbons he has so arduously earned. We eventually lose our identity in our work, and we lose the capacity to relate to anything other than our work. Many a workaholic dies at his desk or shortly after retirement, proud to have served in the only game he ever knew.

The Secret

The secret of work warriors is an overriding emptiness and frustration. Work becomes the vessel into which they pour their self-image, their energy, and their essence. Work warriors are often the ones in the hospital with heart attacks. They are the ones with nervous anxiety, ulcers, and other digestive diseases. They are the ones who miss their son's games, their daughter's competitions, their spouse's fundraisers, or family events. They become a shadow of themselves in their relationships because they are not really present over a lifetime. They are present in name, but they have no substance.

Their emotional commitment is to the work. Their marriages are really made with the job. Their offspring are the projects and tasks they shepherd. Their work becomes their first family, while their human family becomes some distant symbols on a Christmas card.

There is a sadness here. Consider your own memories of your parents. Was your father a "remote dad"? Was your mother a commitment junky who gave to everyone else in the community but not to you as a child? Do you remember the one time your father played ball with you versus all the sports equipment he gave you over the years?

Work-warrior parents are probably well meaning, but the money, the honors, and the recognition they garner as a result of their work come at the sacrifice of being real parents or partners. Their gifts become stand-ins for themselves. And their spouses, their children, their friends, and their community never have access to them as living, breathing people.

The insidious secret of the Workaholic Game is that workaholics have no intimacy with themselves, much less with others. They don't know what their needs or desires are because they've subverted everything into their jobs. They are remote with themselves; they are remote with others. Sometimes it takes a heart attack or a stroke to get them back into their bodies and away from their work. It may be only then that healing and true growth can begin.

Game Triggers

The Workaholic Game can be triggered as early as the preteen years if circumstances or those who influence us force us to believe we have to work harder and harder to feel secure. Interestingly, either failure or success can trigger workaholism. If we fail at a job or don't make enough money, we will get another job or work two jobs or more. Our failure drives our obsession to succeed.

On the other hand, if we succeed at a line of work or profession, we may have a fear of losing the success, and redouble our efforts. We become obsessed with duplicating the success. Above all, this dynamic is motivated by some sort of deep-seated commitment gone askew. We may commit to creating a good income, or raising a family, or taking care of our mate, or sending our kids to college, or providing a good retirement, but when this commitment exceeds everything else at the expense of our mental, emotional, and physical health, it ceases to be a commitment and becomes an obsession.

Workaholism taken to its extreme is an obsessive-compulsive need to control. Work fills up the empty, fear-saturated spaces in an individual's life, even if that individual's life includes lots of people and many circumstances that require him or her to engage with others. Workaholism happens when we feel a lack of control, and our anxiety about it starts to engulf us. We turn to our sheer will to work and thus keep the fear at bay. We use work as a shield to protect us from the fear of failing and perhaps annihilation.

Failure fears can get triggered in any number of situations:

- A family-owned business begins to falter
- A parent who owns a business brings up sons or daughters to take over, and one becomes the "good child" because he sacrifices himself to the work
- Adult children of abusing parents are raised to believe they are "lazy, stupid, and will never amount to anything," and this becomes the adult's work ethic for disproving the parent
- A child becomes gravely ill
- An adult child lost his or her parents at a young age due to tragedy or illness
- A person witnesses tragic loss of resources (house or land burns down, family files for bankruptcy)

- A spouse or partner abandons you for someone more successful
- Divorce or death of family members
- Financial reversal
- Recovery from drug, alcohol, or other addictions
- Need to escape from something else (bad marriage, conflict with children, family illness, etc.)

Disarming Strategies

To disarm workaholism, take a look at how you are spending your time and seek more balance. Take a close look at how much you are spending to feed your workaholic habit.

Consider making a list of your personal priorities: work, family life, education, personal time, recreation, et cetera. Note where you are putting most of your energy. Then, next to the priority, put a percentage for how much of your time and energy go to this area.

For each of these priorities, answer these questions in writing:

- What's the payoff for spending my time and energy here?
- What am I giving up to put my time here?
- How will I feel in ten years if I look back and realize I've spent this much time here?
- Who am I sacrificing in my life in order to fulfill my obsession?
- Who or what is secretly driving my need to do or be this?
- Am I ready to tell my "controllers" to take a hike and take back my life?

Another strategy is to visualize your ideal day if you had no worries, no priorities, and no pressure. Write out what it would look like, what you would be doing and feeling. Now see if there is some way you can merge the two realities—your ideal day and your real day—together. Begin to make a plan for "getting more of your ideal in your real."

Your New Way of Thinking

"I see work as a means to an end, not the end itself. I am not my job. Those who care about me—family and friends—love me unconditionally for who I am, not what I do. I own the work; it does not own me."

Your Action Plan

Inner steps to take:

1. Create a pie chart of your time over a year. Allocate percentages for work, play, family, children, self-improvement, sleep, vacation, and so on. If work is more than one-third of the 8,760 hours in a year, you may want to consider whether you are a workaholic and whether you want to consider living your life with more balance.

2. Write a eulogy for yourself as you think your children might write it, using at least 100 words. Consider if this is the legacy you want to leave.

3. Instead of buying Christmas presents (or instead of buying *too many* presents) this year, encourage everybody in your family to list twenty-five reasons why the recipient is loved or valued. (Twenty-five is a lot of reasons, so the writers are sure to come up with some off-the-wall expressions as well as deep, genuine ones.) But, for you, the number or quality of the reasons won't be as important as the source of the plaudits.

   How many relate to you as breadwinner? As a hard worker? As someone who bears great responsibility at work? If those roles are what you're primarily valued for, are you spending too much time on those and not enough on something else?

4. Create a list of the most important experiences you have had in your life and see how many relate to money and work. Which do you need more of?

5. Create a list of the most important experiences you *want* to have in your life. How many revolve around work or money? If you concentrated on the nonwork, nonmoney ones, how would your life change? Do you want it to change in that manner?

6. Pursue some new hobbies or diversions—say, learning to really play the guitar well or perhaps hiking the Appalachian Trail—that you haven't had time for. Or if that is too ambitious, make a date to go camping or for a bike ride with your friends or family.

7. Ask your partner/family members what activities they most enjoy that don't require money and don't create stress for them. You may be surprised at the answers. For example, they may say playing catch in the backyard or talking or taking long walks. Whatever the answer, make the time to do it.

Financial steps to take:

1. The average work-year is 2,000 man-hours (50 weeks × 40 hours). But add to that the number of hours you spent last year working overtime and on weekends. Then add to that your commuting and travel time. What figure do you come up with? Twenty-five hundred hours? Three thousand? More? Divide that figure into your yearly salary for a true hourly wage.

   Are you comfortable with expending that much of your life for that amount of money? After taxes, how much of that extra money is really spendable? What do you buy with it? Is what you buy with the extra money of equal or greater value than what you're giving up in terms of lost time to enjoy yourself, to be with your family, to follow your passions? Does that extra time working come with a cost to your health, your peace of mind, your relationships? What figure would you put on that?

2. Take one unscheduled day off from work this month and call it your own. Do something you'd never do during the

week: Go to a museum. Or for a sail. Or just do nothing much at all but seek to soothe your harried heart and over-wrought mind by, say, watching a sunset, tasting an éclair, grabbing a nap, or going to the beach, the mountains, or the woods. Decline to do anything on this day that has to do with work or money. And next month, try this for two days.

Think about It

"Most luxuries and many of the so-called comforts of life are not only not indispensable, but positive hindrances to the elevation of mankind."

—Henry David Thoreau

THE WORKAHOLIC GAME	
Rules	The burden's on me. I have to produce, produce, produce. If I don't, I'm a failure.
Belief	I have to work, work, and work to keep feeling fulfilled and to keep others satisfied.
Secret	I despise being trapped in this role, but I can't seem to stop.
Feeling	Fear, resentment, despair
Game Triggers	Fear of failure, family pressure, family tragedy, obsession, need to control to feel good, need to escape into work
Disarming Strategies	Assess priorities and what you are gaining/giving up to be a workaholic.
Persona	Atlas
Action	Know thyself, set appropriate priorities, live in balance.

Chapter Seven

Game #5: The Bag Lady Game

Andy's Story

Andy and his wife, Ann, first came to see me about investments their previous financial advisor had placed them in. Putting all of their money into stocks was too scary, and they felt overly exposed to risk. They both had grown up in lower-middle- to middle-class families. Andy described growing up having enough food and clothes, but not much money for extras. Ann's family was always cared for financially, but with little money left over for vacations and extras.

As a couple, Andy and Ann lived frugally even though Andy made $100,000 a year. After making a significant contribution to his savings plan each month, Andy put all the rest back into his company. Ann stayed at home in search of the right job. They had two boys, nine and eleven. Both Andy and Ann were college graduates, but neither appeared to be happy. Andy believed his children should be able to get by on a minimal amount of money. Andy and Ann, who taught their children to be thrifty, became annoyed when the children wanted every new toy that flashed by on television.

Andy and Ann dutifully believed, as had their parents and

grandparents before them, that saving money is a virtue. Andy's parents especially had railed against those who were money mongers; Andy's farmer father repeatedly had been forced to go to the bank for loans after his crops failed. He grew to hate the lenders, and that hatred seeped out into the family. He always admonished his sons to maintain their financial solvency and "never give in to the evil money doers." As a child, Andy used to have nightmares about the "evil money men" coming to take their furniture and car away; sometimes he'd wet the bed during these dreams. Andy's bed-wetting didn't stop until he got his first job at age eleven at the local market as a packer and he got his first few dollars in his pocket. "It was a relief not to be so poor," he told me.

Ann's family home was repossessed when she was twelve because her father lost his butcher job. She recalled living in a trailer park for a few years. "It was so humiliating having to walk to school; everyone knew we lived in a trailer and I had to sew all my own clothes." After a few years, Ann's parents were able to buy another home, but Ann told me, "I never forgot the humiliation."

When they married, Andy and Ann made a pact. They agreed to be careful with their money—always. They told each other they would never bring their children up to be afraid about money. They decided then and there to save at least 15 percent of their income a year and take vacations only every three years. They decided to dedicate themselves to family sports, but agreed to limit those activities to inexpensive sports like family baseball and basketball.

Typically, Andy worked twelve-hour days in his business, a computer software–design company. Ann was left to take care of the family most of the time. She spent her time cleaning, canning, sewing clothes, and clipping coupons. On weekends, Andy was usually at work, trying to nudge his latest product to the market before his competition. Both parents pushed their children into school sports "so you can get a scholarship to college." The family deferred spending whenever it could; over ten years, the only vacations they took were trips to the mountains every few years to pick apples and camp in a tent. The family ate out only once a month (if that), and the boys never tasted fast food until they were in high school.

When the two boys were sixteen and eighteen, the technology bubble burst and Andy's business went bankrupt. The hundreds of thousands of dollars that they had plowed religiously back into Andy's business were virtually wiped out overnight. The 15 percent savings they had socked away year after year was their only cushion. A short time later, Andy had a heart attack. Ann felt she had to go back to work despite their nest egg, which now was nearly $225,000. Despite her college degree, she took a menial job in a sewing-material store and went home daily to care for Andy, who recovered after a year of bed rest. Soon, one of his inventions took off in the technology market. A Japanese company purchased his computer security protection software for $500,000, but Andy banked it all, continuing to worry for the future.

The boys both took part-time jobs and later each went to an inexpensive junior college. After both sons were married, Andy and Ann considered their options for retirement in a few years and came to see me. Both looked haggard and worn, despite being only in their mid-fifties. They spoke about feeling impoverished but wanting to invest what little money they did have in their retirement. I was shocked to learn that their nest egg was now $1.5 million, but the couple still was clipping coupons, saving on expenses, canning, growing vegetables in the backyard, and never taking vacations out of the state. Both said they were realizing now that "we have never really enjoyed our lives. We have been so frugal, we have never really enjoyed what we have."

We began to discuss the couple's core safety values. They agreed they had saved at all cost. The couple told me that they felt that "money is sacred and we really have needed to watch our pennies or there wouldn't be enough when we really needed it." Ann added, "Even with our money, we worry about it, not having enough. We feel out of control. And then Andy's nightmares return. I am so afraid he will have another heart attack and then I'll be alone."

After a time, each admitted being terrified of ending up in the same kind of financial straits their parents had experienced. Despite Ann and Andy's obvious wealth, they began to realize they had sacrificed all levels of comfort to feel safe. Over several meetings we also began to explore the issue of hypersaving behavior as disguised greed. We also came up with a prudent investment plan and helped the couple put a little aside for relaxation and vacation time.

Sadly, after a year of planning a more enjoyable future, Andy had another heart attack. Within a month, he died. Ann came to see me later that year. She told me, "He never really got to enjoy his life very much. We were planning that cruise for next spring, but we never got to take it. It would have been our thirtieth wedding anniversary." Her eyes filled with tears. "We always lived for the future, scrimping and saving. Now we have plenty of money to enjoy the rest of our lives, but Andy is gone. If I leave my sons with only one thought, it will be: Live a little more for today, since you really don't know how long you have." $

The Bag Lady Game: When Saving Turns to Hoarding

The Bag Lady Game is played by well-meaning people who are always trying to "get enough" to feel safe with their money. The problem is the feeling of being out of control and not having enough money to be in control. It doesn't matter how much you save or put away. It still can't make that desperate feeling of primal fear disappear.

No matter how much they saved, Andy and Ann still felt compelled to tighten their spending. Prudent saving behavior becomes an obsession when we hoard money at the expense of our own comfort and well-being. At a surface level, players keep close tabs on their money, typically fending off the attempts of others to deplete their funds. If they have a partner or child who spends money more freely, they will typically use judgment and overmoralization to control the other person's spending. To control their own anxiety with money, they may resort to threatening, using unprovoked guilt, and blaming those family members who don't see eye to eye with them on implementation of an ironclad budget and savings plan.

Bag Lady people are often the last ones to pick up the tab at a group lunch. They will be the chronic bargain shoppers (when they shop at all), the lifelong coupon clippers, and the family "tightwads."

Their game is to control whatever they have, be it funds, furniture, cars, clothes, food, and more. They may also be pack-rat types who won't get rid of anything, even if it's thirty years old. They take great pride in their ingenuity and cleverness in outsmarting others with bargains. Being able to purchase a new outfit that came from a thrift store and looks like a designer creation is tallied as a major victory. These individuals appear self-assured and self-confident, but underneath, they are scared to death of not having enough and feel just one step away from poverty.

The Belief

The Bag Lady Game is played from a deep belief in needing to hoard what we have. Bag Lady people are stuck in deep safety, security, and basic survival needs at the exclusion of all others. After the stock market dropped drastically from 2000 to 2002, many moved into a Bag Lady mentality. When people feel they can't count on the certainty of their retirement account due to market volatility, they may find themselves believing that they must save and pull in the reins or end up destitute.

Many with this belief had parents or grandparents who suffered in the Great Depression. They can vividly recount, word for word, descriptions of parents' or grandparents' tales of barely getting by financially. Many have heard these paralyzing stories repeatedly at family gatherings. They can end up with a warped, fear-driven mindset toward money. Having lived with horror stories of the Depression, they fear it happening again. In today's world, when we live in a grasping mode based on fear, we participate in a poverty consciousness. Thinking that we won't have enough money is debilitating, and it can lead to hoarding.

We may find ourselves stocking up on food, not spending even on necessities, and putting our saving needs ahead of all others. When money and resources come to us, we stop the flow. It dams up when it hits our coffers. We do not participate in the flow of money life. We stop our own joy, our own enjoyment, our own pleasure.

By living life under these restrictions, we probably feel more stress, negativity, and unhappiness. Most of us who live with this mind-set experience a lack of fulfillment. We miss out on the normal give-and-take that exists when this fear is absent. The Bag Lady Game is one that manifests in compulsive behavior. Players say they can't turn off their thinking about how to scrimp. They are constantly on the lookout for new ways to save. Some players comment on how no matter what, they won't touch their principal investment. If they do, they believe they will soon find themselves destitute. They will avoid this at all costs, even if it means having to eat cat food or visit a soup kitchen for meals.

The Secret

At a deeper level, the Bag Lady Game is about greed. It's about having more than someone else because we come first at all costs. We deny our own human-fulfillment needs to satisfy the monster that is greed. We mask our grasping by patting ourselves on the back for being so prudent, so wise. But the reality is, when we stop the flow, we are starving ourselves and others. As our bank accounts grow fat, we starve our own human need to participate in the flow of life. We choke the positive energy of abundance by stopping up the flow for ourselves. Our coffers can become our coffins.

Game Triggers

Triggers for the Bag Lady Game are everywhere, particularly in today's economy. When investments go down and there are rumors of war, when layoffs abound and the financial future is uncertain, many of us move into Bag Lady mode. Some other triggers for the Bag Lady Game include:

- A past failure with money
- A family belief system based around money fear

- Past money success combined with recent money failure
- Economic uncertainty
- Rumors of shortages (water, canned goods, household staples, etc.)
- Investments based on someone else's advice gone sour
- Bankruptcy
- Divorce and economic hardship
- Birth of a child
- Aging, illness, or death
- Lack of earning potential from downsizing of career industry
- Lack of ability to learn new skills (computers, online investing, money management)

Disarming Strategies

Disengaging from the Bag Lady Game can be done in small or large steps. It's a question of increasing prudent risk taking and managing financial anxiety.

One way to begin disengaging from Bag Lady behavior is to create a "Money Fear Hierarchy"—"If this . . . then this will happen"—regarding your money beliefs. The hierarchy will look something like this:

Money Fear Hierarchy (sample)

If I don't save money . . . Then I will end up penniless.

If I end up penniless . . . Then I will end up alone and on the street.

If I end up alone and on the street . . . Then I will feel ashamed about how I handled money.

If I feel ashamed about how I handled money . . . Then I will consider myself a complete failure.

If I feel I am a complete failure . . . Then I will not be able to live with myself.

If I feel like I can't live with myself for my failures . . . Then I will have to admit that I base my value on my ability to generate money.

(Continue with your own hierarchy.)

If I feel . . . Then I . . .

Continue until you have explored all your money fears.

A second step is to create a "Money Comfort Hierarchy." It will look something like this:

Money Comfort Hierarchy (sample)

If I can stop hoarding all my money ... Then I might be able to give up some of my money fear and become more comfortable.

If I give up some of my money fear ... Then I might be able to come up with a more balanced saving and spending plan.

If I come up with a more balanced saving and spending plan ... Then I will feel like I can both save money and reward myself.

If I can learn to both save and reward myself ... Then I may be able to feel good about others both saving and rewarding themselves.

If I feel good about others' saving and spending ... Then I may not need to control my money around them nor will I need to control them.

If I feel like I don't have to control so much, I might feel freer with myself and others ... Then I might be able to relax and my money anxiety will decrease.

(Continue with your own hierarchy.)

If I feel ... Then I ...

Once you've explored both your money-fear and money-comfort hierarchies, draft a plan to disengage from the fear statements and embrace the comfort statements.

Your New Way of Thinking

"I reject the urge to be selfish and fearful with my money, saving it all for myself, and I will now act with the goodwill of all in mind. I place my complete trust in the universe so that if I act with the right motives, all will turn out well in my life."

Your Action Plan

Inner steps to take:

1. Check to see that you aren't coming from a place of fear and scarcity when you save. Put aside enough for emergencies and retirement, but don't deprive yourself of what you and your partner/family need.

2. Talk with your friends about this syndrome. It's so common

that some of them probably are familiar with it as well. Knowing that others share it may lessen its hold on you.

3. Write your eulogy as you think your children might write it, using at least 100 words. Consider if this is the legacy you want to leave.

4. Create a list of the most important experiences you have had in your life and see how many relate to work and money.

5. Create a list of the most important experiences you want to have. How many involve money or work? If you concentrated on the nonmoney, nonwork ones, how would your life change? Do you want it to change in that manner?

6. Work with a therapist to examine your money background. Is fear a learned family trait? Use the Money History Assessment at the end of Chapter 4.

7. Find a new money mantra. Say instead, "I am affluent enough to enjoy life, and I will."

8. Volunteer at a homeless shelter. Becoming familiar with the existing support networks may help quell your fears that no such mechanisms exist.

9. Remember Horace Vandergelder's words in the Broadway musical, *Hello Dolly!*: "Money is like manure; it's made to be spread around." Viewing money as something that is simply meant to circulate, you can see that it is inefficient to hoard huge amounts of it out of fear. This means that, by acting responsibly with money—avoiding either extreme of spending or hoarding—you can live a life of balance.

Financial steps to take:

1. Once a month, take a specific amount of money and spend it impulsively on yourself.

2. Once a month, go out and spend money on a small luxury for someone you love.

3. Ignore your budget or your bank account for three months. Don't make a budget and don't open your bank or brokerage statements.

4. Establish a relationship with a financial counselor, whether a CPA, a financial planner, or some other professional. Meet regularly (monthly perhaps at first, then quarterly, then yearly) so he or she can assure you that you're doing OK with your money and need not fret.

Think about It

"Remember that you ought to behave in life as you would at a banquet. As something is being passed around it comes to you; stretch out your hand, take a portion of it politely. It passes on; do not detain it. Or it has not come to you yet; do not project your desire to meet it, but wait until it comes in front of you. So act toward children, so toward a wife, so toward office, so toward wealth."

—Epictetus

THE BAG LADY GAME	
Rules	Save as much as I can, never spend, never give anything away.
Belief	I have to save or I'll be broke before I know it and out on the street.
Secret	The world is a fearful place and I can't count on anyone or anything if things get bad. I don't trust anything but my money. I don't believe in pleasure but I sure do miss it.
Feeling	Mistrust, terror, constriction
Game Triggers	Money fears, economic downturn, fuzzy financial future, life changes or tragedies, marriage, divorce, childbirth, illness
Disarming Strategies	Confront fears, affirm money comfort, embrace financial balance.
Persona	Pack Rat, Bag Lady
Action	Strive for balance between saving and spending. Reward yourself and practice giving to balance your need to conserve.

Chapter Eight

Game #6: The Got-More Game

Jerry's Story

Jerry worked as an independent software consultant when I met him. His office was in the same building as mine. Jerry always seemed to be in motion. He was forever jetting off to some island resort with his partner, or acquiring the latest high-tech gizmo. As he told me one evening, however, he was troubled. Even though he was constantly making big expenditures, he was finding it more and more difficult to make it financially. The conflict between keeping up with the Joneses and surviving financially was taking its toll on Jerry.

Out of the blue, Jerry announced he was going to move his office into his home. Then a few months later, he decided to have his partner go back to work. When we had dinner a couple of weeks later, he and his partner told me they now had a thirty-foot Bayliner boat at Lake Mead near Las Vegas, a brand-new Ford Excursion, and a completely remodeled home in La Jolla. Jerry's beautifully coiffed partner was wearing the latest designer fashions. During dessert, however, they complained about how stressed they were because Jerry had maxed out several VISA and MasterCard accounts.

Later that week in a private meeting, I asked Jerry if he was doing all right. He opened his heart up to me. He said, "Hey, I'm just living the American dream, Tom. But I think it's killing me." He went on to tell me that it had all begun in junior high school for him. "That's when I started measuring myself against other boys—in the locker room, you know, before physical education." He said he noticed that some of the boys were more developed than he was, and he hated it.

Jerry said that, right then and there, he devised a plan of action. He started working out and eating better so his body would mature more quickly. He said he watched and learned that kids with better tennis shoes could run a little faster, "that is, if they also had talent," he explained. He also noticed that "kids who were dressed better seemed to be treated better. They got more privileges, more stuff, better treatment. I knew then that I was always going to have my best foot forward from that day on," he told me with a big smile.

A few months later, Jerry told me he was going to have to liquidate his retirement accounts to start paying off his debts. Jerry admitted to me that he was finally realizing how devastating the Money Game he had been playing had been for him. Jerry had just refinanced his house, using the money he pulled out to pay off the contractor who did the remodeling and who was threatening legal action. Jerry was cut off by the credit-card companies when they realized he was simply rolling over his debt and supplementing his lifestyle with eleven credit cards totaling over $200,000 in debt. His line of credit at the bank was used up, and Jerry was at the end of his rope financially.

Jerry was stunned when he finally saw how negative his financial picture was. He filed for bankruptcy, thinking that was the only way out. Embarrassed and ashamed at how poorly he had played the Money Game, he then suffered the humiliation of surrender. Jerry figured out that life wasn't as fun as it was supposed to be when based on accumulating things he couldn't pay for. He and his partner had to start using cashier's checks to pay their bills. They moved into an apartment. Jerry finally decided to limit his expenditures and stop measuring himself against others. Currently,

Jerry is now in his early sixties and living a more moderate life in Los Angeles, doing sales for a computer company, although he says he still catches himself trying to keep up with the Joneses. $

The Got-More Game: Winning at All Costs

The Got-More Game is a take-no-prisoners battle we wage against each other (and ourselves) as measured by the amount, quantity, and value of our material possessions and worth. Some play this game subtly. Others play it brashly and flashily. You will be familiar with this game if you think twice about the kind of car you drive or the house you can afford because you are compelled to "trade up" constantly. You'll also hear yourself bragging about the last big vacation you took, and you won't be able to stop from letting all your business friends know you made a killing on the stock market last month.

Got-More is a one-upmanship game. There is usually only one winner; the rest of the players will be "losers." The game will always be to score—and score big. When you get to the height of this game, you'll get casual about how much money you make. You'll drop lines like, "If you can count your money, you don't have a billion dollars" (J. Paul Getty). Or you'll show that you have so much money that now you're bored with it: "Money was never a big motivation for me, except as a way to keep score. The real excitement is playing the game" (Donald Trump).

The Belief

The belief behind the Got-More Game is a deep need to win. Accumulation is the yardstick for worth, and players of this game need more and more to retain their money virility. Ego esteem is based on how much more wealth they've got compared to the next player. However, it will be measured not only in net worth, but with the money power they have to vanquish others in the game.

This is a buy-and-conquer dynamic. It's akin to knights tilting in a medieval battlefield. But in the modern commerce arena, players come armed with margin accounts and lines of credit, and use gross values of assets instead of swords. They measure their might by material possessions instead of inches of steel. They come riding in on a Rolls-Royce instead of a stallion. Instead of winning a medal or a crown, they'll get listed on the top-20 moneymakers list. They will be revered for their financial conquests and feared for their money power. They'll get the best restaurant tables, special tickets to events, complimentary goodies, and be quoted in the local financial pages. Might will make them right.

But it can be lonely at the top of the money heap. An offshoot of the Got-More Game is the Got-More Power Game. In the Got-More Power version, we enjoy our money a lot. But we enjoy our power more. Charlie is a case in point.

Charlie's Story

A client of mine named Charlie used to be number four in command of a *Fortune* 500 company. I started working with Charlie toward the end of his life. During his entire career, this man had held out his money as power and demanded that others snap to attention and follow his command. He forced his lieutenants to do his dirty work and often required unethical behavior from his subordinates as the price they paid "to brush with power."

Charlie had alienated almost everybody in his life. This included his own family to the point that his own children didn't talk to him. The few people in Charlie's life were those he did business with, those who were employed by him, or others who were also into the Got-More Power Game. Unfortunately, I don't react well to being ordered around by a Got-More Power Game player, so Charlie and I had some conflict.

During one of my money-consultation sessions with him, I chose to take things personally. Charlie started in on one of his money-power tirades. He made threats to transfer his account to another broker when I wouldn't tolerate his abuse. Sometimes I would make negative comments back to him—participating in my own Got-More Power Game. I have to admit that once I was so vindictive as to put Charlie on speakerphone so my colleagues could hear the tongue-lashings he would dole out. At times we had to mute the phone to prevent him from hearing us laughing.

After we skirmished for a while and I began my own money psychology work, I realized that playing this game wasn't helping either Charlie or me. I admitted that it was a losing proposition for both of us. I had to swallow my pride and realize that this is how Charlie treated everyone in the world and that it had worked well for him.

Eventually Charlie found that the idle threats to transfer his account no longer worked with me. I told him he would have to be civil to me or I wouldn't respond to him. When I finally got to the point that Charlie's money power over me wasn't enough to captivate me, the game ended. He began treating me like another human being.

Eventually Charlie passed away. I believe he would have been extremely upset that almost no one came to his funeral. There was a smattering of close family members, one or two business associates, and me. It seemed a sad, sparse tribute to him. But Charlie had made his life with his money power. In death, it had deserted him. $

The Secret

For both Jerry and Charlie, the secret of the game is that there's no end to it. There will always be people with bigger toys, more power. Consider the pressure of pledging to have the newest, largest, and most sophisticated big-screen television, for example. We have to stay glued to the Internet, scan the newest technical magazines, and be ready to purchase that television as soon as it is available, even though we know it will cost half as much if we waited for a year or even six months to buy it.

A person who uses money and money power as a means to empower himself over others creates a divisive act. When we stoop to the level of using our income, job title, or financial assets to rule over others, we've entered onto an ugly playing field. Most of us only resort to this type of behavior as a last-ditch effort to use money power as a trump card. If we get money power in an authentic way with integrity, we gain support as we evolve. If we evolve our power by stepping on and over others, we create a great band of enemies along the way.

The Got-More Game takes a lot of time and energy. Fortifying our position can consume us. The game can suck every ounce of soul out of us. Focusing on a target that carries with it the illusion that "I have arrived," is, in fact, a mirage. The secret is that we, in fact, will never fully arrive if our only goal is money power.

Money power is a transitory illusion. But what's real are the enemies we create and the bloated target we become as we slash our way to wealth. We'll feel like we have to defend our power positions, and we *will* be right. There's only one winner in this game. And we'll have vanquished any possible allies. We'll stand alone and unprotected. And we are justified in our fear. Any winner-takes-all power monger who believes his own myth is ripe for a takeover.

Game Triggers

Got-More Games are sometimes triggered by the mere smell of money power. More than a survival dynamic or a safety measure, money power becomes the ultimate ego trip. In fact, the feeling probably comes from the adrenaline rush we get when we sense there's a challenge to our power. In ancient days, this adrenaline rush surged when the challenge came in the form of a wild animal heading toward us with its jaws open. The adrenaline served us well as a primitive way of preserving our lives.

Today, we have few outlets for that hormonal blast. But the emotions remain the same. We feel challenged, we get afraid, we get angry in our fear, we want to attack for fear of being vanquished first. But standing before us is not a prehistoric beast but a deal to be done. There's plenty of evidence to suggest that the new Roman Coliseum is, in fact, the worldwide stock exchange, where the Christians (investors) and the lions (the volatility of the stock market) are still doing bloody battle. Out of the ancient emotions comes the hormonal blast. And we are at war.

Another aspect of the adrenaline blast is that it makes us "high." We get a high from fear reactions. Once we overcome the initial discomfort, we learn to like it. We enjoy the rush. Sometimes we create events to get it. In sports, aggression becomes an appropriate outlet. In money matters, vanquishing our money enemies can become our cocaine, our heroin. When we have become money power junkies, we get high on the power and feel empty, unfulfilled, and wilted if we are forced to the sidelines.

When we feel threatened, challenged, or "low" after having money power, the game easily retriggers us. Common triggers include:

- Being reared by an aggressive parent who taught you "winner takes all" games
- Being chided into playing one-up, one-down games as a child or teen, then being rewarded or punished for your results
- Naively entering a business deal and getting taken advantage of
- Innocently entering a marital arrangement and getting taken advantage of
- Going through a nasty divorce where money is the key issue
- Losing your shirt in a financial situation because you were too nice
- Watching your family business get taken over by aggressors
- Wanting to get ahead and watching people who misuse their power to win
- Believing you have to be conniving to be rich
- Needing the high to keep going and finding life dull without having a "deal to do"

Disarming Strategies

Moving out of the Got-More Game can take some soul-searching. You may not want to give it up. If you get charged up while you play it, you may find it hard to disengage from the field of play. But if you have heart stress, hypertension, or high blood pressure; if you experience a heart attack or stroke; or if your loved ones have all abandoned you, then you may be ready to consider that there may be more to life. This game can literally kill you.

One disarming strategy is to envision a famous money power broker, like Donald Trump, George Soros, or Rupert Murdoch. Write down everything you admire about him or her. Then read your description aloud. Note how you feel as you read it. Do you desire these qualities? Are they benchmarks for how you live your life?

Another strategy is to write down on ten to thirty large sticky notes everything that excites you, one idea per sticky note. Then post these on the wall in two groups: "Can Live Without" and "Can't Live Without." Be honest with yourself. See what it would take to move each of the "Can't Live Withouts" to the "Can Live Without" column. If you can't move them all, you may be addicted to the act. If it's with money power, you are probably off balance in your personal priorities and source of personal power.

Your New Way of Thinking

"I will learn to love what I have. When I liberate myself from thinking that I need to have more than others to be happy, I will discover the freedom and joy that come from being content with what I already possess."

Your Action Plan

Inner steps to take:

1. Commit to balancing your power needs. Using your money power profile from the assessment at the end of this chapter, come up with an alternative plan of action. But avoid beating yourself up and taking the completely opposite stance. In other words, don't give up all your money in

order to become a "money saint." That's just another form of extreme behavior.

2. Think about how else you could use your personal power and channel your assertiveness. Perhaps taking up a competitive sport—say, kick boxing, boxing, karate, rock climbing, surfing, or snow boarding—would be helpful. The physical contact may create a release of that primal survival state that has inadvertently been channeled into this Money Game. Other, less physically threatening yet still competitive sports such as racing, hunting, or fishing also may work. Any activity that externalizes your power in a healthy way would be a good substitute. Also, monitor how you deal with your emotions like anger. If you don't handle your anger in a nonthreatening way, take an anger management class.

3. Channel your personal power by helping your community. For example, chair a committee for fundraising for the local homeless shelter or other needy organization. But be sure you do it for community service rather than personal aggrandizement.

4. Share your power with others by teaching at a local institution, coaching a business group, or becoming a mentor. If you have strong business experience, investigate the Senior Corps of Retired Executives (SCORE), a nationwide nonprofit group that mentors small-business people. Again, be sure you are giving back in healthy ways, not as a power play.

5. Educate your partner/kids about how a planned adventure, like a backpacking trip, could take the place of having to purchase that new powerboat or the latest high-tech television.

6. Spend some time with real people who aren't power brokers. Find out what excites them. Try some of their approaches to life and broaden your horizons.

7. Take up tai chi, meditation, or, for that matter, fly-fishing as a means of getting past the superficial allure of money and possessions.

Financial steps to take:

1. Allow people in your life to take the financial steering wheel once in a while. Try the backseat by letting them decide about major expenditures and investments. Taking a step back may give you time to decompress and perhaps come up with even better ideas.

2. Before you seal your next deal, purchase your next investment, or make that next big purchase, take a few minutes to think about your motive. If you are taking the action out of a need to feel powerful or get "high," consider the cost. Of course, if the transaction has real, long-term benefit to you, go ahead. But if it's only a momentary high, consider passing. The point is to decide from a nonemotional place whether to proceed or withdraw. Take a rational approach and stop letting your emotions/hormones control you.

3. Give back 10 percent of your wealth or energy or talent anonymously. Do it without regard for recognition or reward.

4. Try to live for one month in a state of austerity, then write about your experiences.

5. Find a picture of yourself when you were in high school. Look at it and reflect on how you have changed. Ask yourself what qualities you formerly had that you liked, and then take positive action to reinforce those forgotten qualities. Participate in activities that support the positive aspects of who you were. For instance, maybe you used to toss darts or practice archery or play handball or horseshoes. Revisiting those pastimes might be beneficial.

6. Rent or borrow an older car and drive it for a month or two. Experience how you are treated differently.

Think about It

"He that loveth silver shall not be satisfied with silver, nor he that loveth abundance with increase."

—Ecclesiastes 5:10

THE GOT-MORE GAME

Rules	Whoever has the most stuff or money power wins.
Belief	If I have more than you, I'm better than you and I have more power than you do.
Secret	The game never ends and I always have to watch my back. Additional secret: I get high on the power.
Feeling	Insecurity, paranoia, impotence
Game Triggers	Being threatened, former money or family abuse, getting taken advantage of, feeling victimized in money transactions, feeling empty without a money power play to make
Disarming Strategies	Consider your addictions, get centered, realign your priorities.
Persona	Attila the Hun
Action	Use your power positively. Give up winning at all cost; enjoy the view from the backseat once in a while.

Money Power Assessment

After the following statements, write *T* for those that are true for you, and *F* for those that are false.

1. My life is complicated financially and I have to stay on top of it. ____

2. Frankly, people who don't understand money bore me a little. ____

3. I honestly believe the most powerful people in the world are the rich. ____

4. I use money to measure myself against others. ____

5. I have daydreams about being more rich and powerful. ____

6. If I want to impress someone, I let it slip how much money I have. ____

7. I have sometimes won arguments because I have more money and, as a result, know more. ____

8. I think when people lose money as in a bankruptcy, they lose power. ____

9. Without money I'm a failure. ____

10. I use my money to get what I want in life. ____

11. When people with more money than me talk, I listen. ____
12. If I had more money I'd be happier. ____
13. I worry about money and strategize how to make more and more of it. ____
14. I can't let my guard down; I have to be using every waking minute of every day to get ahead. ____
15. I often do research on how to make more money even while on vacation. ____

If you answered more than six of these as true, you may be playing a Money Power Game.

Chapter Nine

Game #7: The Old Money Game

Ted's Story

Ted was retired when I was introduced to him. He was transplanted from New York, where he had owned several office buildings and apartments. Ted came from a very wealthy New York family and had made many millions through his own investments. Ted's father always lectured him about how his own father came from nothing, but how hard work and money had earned the family the respect it deserved. "Just remember, Ted, we own people. They tried to keep us down when we first got to this country, but now we own half the city. Always remember that. We deserve respect—we earned it. Never let anybody treat you like scum."

Ted had moved from New York to retire in Lake Arrowhead, California. Ted and his wife had selected this community in which to retire because it was an isolated area situated at 6,000 feet, with a population of a few thousand people. Los Angeles was a two- to three-hour drive from Ted's new home.

The reason I mention where Ted lived is that you need to understand that coming from Manhattan, he was probably doomed to be bored. Ted was not an outdoorsman. He loved being from the

111

East Coast, hobnobbing with all the important, influential people there.

Ted was now a "big fish" living in a "small pond" in Lake Arrowhead. This soon became a problem. He had very little to do except occasionally drive into Los Angeles for some culture or, as he put it, to "get on the phone to get the respect I deserve." Ted's wife, Lee, would constantly tell me, "Ted is driving me up the wall now that he's retired. I can't wait for the days when he drives up to Las Vegas to play craps so I can breathe."

Ted loved these trips to Vegas where he felt he was treated with respect since "I throw so much money around." Ted told me about how he was given a suite at the Hilton where he liked to stay. Ted said, "It isn't that I have to have the best money can buy. I just want respect." To Ted, this meant that the hotel staff knew him by his first name, the pit boss treated him to shows and had dinner with him, and in general he got preferential treatment. This was what Ted said he had lived for.

My relationship with Ted was one based on deference as well. Ted liked to have me drive up to his home once each quarter to present the latest update on his $10 million portfolio. As long as I scheduled the meetings and made the trip to have dinner with Ted and his wife, Ted felt respected. Respect to Ted also meant that, religiously at 8 A.M. every Wednesday, I would call him. We would spend one hour covering the latest happenings in the municipal bond and stock markets. Failure to carry out these expectations would cause Ted to give me a sharp tongue-lashing, which usually resulted in his threatening to move his account to another brokerage firm where he would "get some respect."

Ted once told me, "I have more money than 99 percent of the population. I am entitled to the best service and treatment the world has to offer." Unfortunately, all the money in the world couldn't buy perfect health for Ted or his wife. Lee contracted cancer about five years after I started managing their money. Ted quickly lost interest in his money and his entitlement to respect.

He wept over the phone one day. "Tom, I'm losing the most important thing in my life," he said. And for the next several months,

Ted devoted all of his efforts to trying to find a remedy for his wife's illness. He pulled out all the stops, finding the best doctors that money could buy. Lee's cancer was finally arrested. Then, suddenly, when it looked like things were under control, Ted, an avid smoker, contracted lung cancer. He grew very ill very fast. He passed away within weeks.

During the funeral, Ted's children took me aside. They asked me if I thought his rigid nature and demand for respect had led to his death. I told them I thought that all of the anger he cultivated about how he needed others to treat him in the world had a significant impact on his health. All three of his children agreed that they believed that "karma had caught up to our dad." They said, "You can't treat people so meanly and not have it come back to you at some point." All three children had been on the receiving end of his diatribes for not offering their father the proper amount of respect. None of his kids had been close to their dad, and two of them had not spoken to him in the last six months before he was diagnosed with cancer.

Sadly, Ted was now gone. His money had earned him respect, but it also distanced him from family, experiences, and relationships. His anger and resentment kept him from enjoying his wealth. Instead he used it as a weapon, and littered his world with all the people he vanquished with it. $

The Old Money Game: Taking Money for Granted

You may be able to identify with the idea that money entitles you to respect. Even if you were not born into wealth, perhaps you can relate to some time in your life when you suddenly came into a significant amount of money. Remember how it felt to know you had it? Did you move around in the world differently? Were you more cavalier? Did you feel you had something others didn't? Did you think you deserved just a little more respect?

Having money, whether new money or inherited wealth, is like a liquid cocoon, insulating us from day-to-day survival cares.

When we have plenty of money, we leave behind the three basic needs: survival, safety, and belonging. We don't think about bills, and we don't have to belong anywhere unless we want to. We don't have to fit in; people must fit into our lifestyle, if we let them. So we are probably living only at the level of the final two needs in the hierarchy: ego esteem and self-actualization.

Sometimes people with money get stuck at ego esteem. It becomes the supreme Money Game to use money to create a mammoth monument to themselves as the producers of all this wealth. Ted played this game. The demand for respect was always a need to pump up that glorified image.

On another level, endless wealth also can push us toward self-actualization. This need moves even beyond the ego-gratification dynamic. At this stage, we have enough money that we no longer even care if people know about it. We have more money than some small countries; we can do anything we want with it.

At this point, our money can be used for a variety of purposes. We can concentrate on ourselves, pleasuring ourselves until we get to a saturation point where we are basically numb. Barbara Hutton, the Woolworth heiress dubbed "the million-dollar baby" at birth, probably died in this frame of mind. She had had so many husbands, so many jewels, so much property, so many ponies, so much designer clothing, so many furnishings, so many drugs, so much alcohol, and so many failed relationships, that it seemed she literally imploded from satiation. She had too much. Her wealth became her disease, and her curse. In her later years, she tried everything to get rid of it. She would give away her diamond bracelets and tiaras to total strangers at the bar in the Beverly Hills Hotel where she lived. She slowly disintegrated, and she blamed her wealth for never finding the love she craved. She had used her extreme wealth to buy anything and everyone in what was probably a desperate attempt to find peace in her world. Ultimately, her wealth became her poison. And it killed her, exquisitely.

Or we can take a different approach at this no-holds-barred level. I suspect Bill Gates is trying to operate from the self-actualization level. He and his wife, Melissa, have everything they need. He has already passed through ego esteem (which surely he milked as he built Microsoft into the world economic power it is today) to self-actualization, the more altruistic social responsibility level.

Like Barbara Hutton, he's independently wealthy, but he's chosen to circulate his wealth for the greater good. The Bill and Melissa Gates Foundation gives away hundreds of millions of dollars each year to various causes and to promote social change. Instead of using their money to saturate themselves, Bill and Melissa are trying to spread their wealth to help the less fortunate. In a very different way from Ted, the Gateses have chosen also to get respect.

Similarly, George Soros, one of the richest men in the world, now heads more philanthropic projects around the world than he could have imagined back when the thrust of his energy was creating wealth through speculative investing. Now his educational projects about AIDS and about the correct use of money in Third World nations are slowly changing the world and the way that humankind thinks.

Soros has stated that all these past parts of his life are fully integrated into who he is today. Just because we move through a Money Game, doesn't mean that we are finished with it. The Money Game will always be a part of us in that it has taught us an invaluable lesson on how to live our life in a more genuine, authentic, life-centered way.

The Belief

If we handle our wealth with humility and social awareness, we are distancing from the Old Money Game. But if we come from a place of money superiority, abusing people with our money power, then we are entrenched in the Old Money Game power plays. We believe money makes us better than others. We assume the "money posture." We expect others to bend in deference. We demand that people look up to us, and if they don't, we wield our power in negative ways.

The Secret

Be aware that lots of millionaires are very happy with their money. They like it, live well with it, and like what it does for them. They don't have any pathological problems with money and report being generally happy in their lives. These people don't manipulate with their money. They remain centered with it.

The players of the Old Money Game, however, are unhappy in their wealth. Ted, for example, was an angry, demanding man, despite his wealth. His children didn't want to be around him. His wife was glad when got away for a few days. Subordinates lived with his wrath. Ted's behavior is indicative of an Old Money Game player.

The dark secret for players is that the money isn't enough. They aren't satisfied with the money alone. They want the capacity it brings to demand servitude from others. They still have to play a Money Game because their egos and core self-esteem are wrapped up in their wealth and their expectations about what it can do for them.

Old Money Game players aren't quite sure who they are without money. They may question the reality of their relationships if they have any sensitivity at all (not a particularly strong trait in money power players). They may wonder, "Am I loved for my money power or for myself?" If they are wondering about it, then they probably have cause to worry.

Old Money Game players may understand they aren't particularly valued as people. They are valued as people with money. They haven't had to evolve their skills, talents, or ability to connect. Their money does everything for them. It buys them things, people, and loyalty—to a point. But there's a price.

Because they buy loyalty and devotion, they may attract the weak and insecure. And how long are such sycophants going to stick around?

The insidious secret of the Old Money Game player is a lack of self-worth and rage about feeling that way. It's a feeling of "not being enough" despite "having enough." It can show up in self-destruction, like it did with Barbara Hutton, or in bullying people and companies, as Ted did just to prove how powerful he was. Ultimately, the secret may be a deep-seated fear of impotence.

Game Triggers

Triggers for this game are pretty obvious.

- Inheriting sudden wealth and getting an entitlement mentality
- Being raised in wealth and feeling different from those without wealth
- Being challenged on your worth as a human being despite your wealth
- Being challenged by someone who has more than you
- A spouse or child threatening a financial lawsuit
- Getting taken advantage of despite your money

Disarming Strategies

If you love your money power, you will probably not want to give up this game. If you have the self-awareness to see that your money power may be making you ill and paranoid, you may begin the long journey toward quitting this game.

This will be a difficult process. Many Old Money Game players have limited ego-strength, resiliency, or self-awareness independent of their money. They have simply not had to cope with it. They may have to start over in evolving a self that is independent of the money dynamic. If this chapter sounds as if it's describing you, then perhaps you're ready to explore a transition to a more well-rounded you. The first step in disengaging from the Old Money dynamic is to get to know yourself. This means knowing what your dreams, your strengths, your weaknesses, your hopes, your vulnerabilities are, independently from your money. This will help you create a realness as to how you are as a human being. You will become intimate with yourself and begin to explore your authentic thoughts and feelings as separate from your money. Some of the techniques you can use to explore you include:

Keep a daily journal of thoughts and feelings about what you are experiencing each day. These entries should have nothing to do with money. They should be about how you feel about the world as you wake up each day and go to bed each night.

Do a morning and evening assessment of what you gave back for that day. Look at what you had planned to accomplish for the day and review it at night. Consider whether you have connected to yourself or whether you have played a Money Game. Consider whether you have connected to others or whether you have played on your money power with them.

Confront your codependency. You may be surprised to learn that your Money Game springs from a dependent relationship with your money. Just like a cocaine addict, a love junkie, or a participant in a codependent marriage, you have given up your self to your money. If you want to disarm this game, you will need to begin building ego-strength independent of your money persona. One of the ways you can do this is to go out among the general population anonymously and interact for a day or a week or a month without your money. Engage in everyday, mundane activities. Or work in a soup kitchen or crisis center or hospital caregiver ward for a day. Find out how you can contribute without your money.

Ask for feedback. This is a tough one. Ask your family, your spouse, your employees, your servants for feedback about you as a human being. This will take courage. What you hear may not be easy, but it will probably be enlightening. Then go to the Action Plan that follows.

Your New Way of Thinking

"I am a human being, separate and apart from my money. I choose to use my money power wisely. I have the wisdom to know how this must be done."

Your Action Plan

Inner steps to take:

1. Make a commitment to know yourself as a human being. Develop yourself, and find out who you are apart from your wealth. Shun the country club. Instead, test your coping ability by putting yourself in situations where you can't rely on your money or power, such as in competitive sports or in nature.

2. Take up hobbies or outlets that allow you to express who you are without using your money. Try, say, gardening, chess, or hiking. Pursue that hobby for a year as a means of meeting people who have similar interests rather than a connection via money.

3. Make a conscious choice here and now to not harm others by using money for your own selfish purposes. Work with a therapist on self-examination, delving into why you act as you do and how you could learn to have healthier relationships.

4. Take responsibility for what you create around you. If you create destructive relationships around yourself, own up to that and vow to change. Honor people for their competence, and don't disparage them for what you believe is their incompetence.

5. Practice compassion. Learn that art of forgiveness, particularly with yourself.

6. Try out the words, "I'm sorry." Use them with your underlings, too, when you have overstepped the bounds of common courtesy.

7. Volunteer to work in worthy nonprofit organizations but only as a rank-and-file member. Refuse to be on the board of directors or other position of authority.

8. Cut yourself some slack in knowing that change takes time and only through continual monitoring of yourself can you move three steps forward for each step back.

Financial steps to take:

1. Find some way to give back 10 percent of your wealth or energy or talent anonymously. Do it without regard for recognition or reward.

2. Try to live for one month in a state of austerity, then write about your experiences.

3. Ignore your bank and brokerage accounts for three months. Don't even open the statements.

4. Give some money anonymously. Experience giving your money without being known for it or expecting something in return.

5. If you can, set up a nonprofit organization to promote a cause you perceive as worthy. But reject becoming a trustee or having any other decision-making role.

6. Take your next vacation with a group that is going on an adventurous trip to some place you've always wanted to go. Insist on nonluxury accommodations—a tent, perhaps—so you can experience nature.

Think about It

"Circumstances don't make a person, they reveal him."
—Richard Carlson

THE OLD MONEY GAME

Rules	I've got more money, so I am entitled.
Belief	I'm better than you since I have more wealth.
Secret	I am not sure who I am without my money. I mask my insecurity with my money.
Feeling	Entitled, empty, insecure
Game Triggers	Disrespect, feeling used, feeling anger and projecting it outward
Disarming Strategies	Give up your codependent relationship with your money.
Persona	Crown Prince/Princess
Action	Commit to being real with yourself and others. Commit to existing with your money, not because of it.

Chapter Ten

Game #8: The Social Climber Game

Tony's Story

Tony is a young attorney who came from meager beginnings. He'd grown up in a barrio with his aunt and uncle, who operated a family restaurant. Tony's real parents had been killed in an automobile accident when he was three years old.

Even as a young attorney, Tony owned the most expensive suits, drove a Mercedes, and had perfected his English to the point that his Hispanic upbringing was unnoticeable. Tony loved rubbing shoulders with the rich and famous. He told me once he believed deep down that only through having fast cars, an attractive blonde for a wife, and an expensive house in the finest area of town could he consider himself successful.

Tony was ingenious at worming his way into what he called "the right social situations" so he could meet "the right kind of people." Tony had few friends from his boyhood. All his new friends were Anglos and "comers" in the financial community. Sometimes when they were partying, Tony would confide in them, "While you white boys are asleep on the job, I am going to fast-talk my way into a sweet situation with the very, very rich. Just watch me."

Tony worked at this plan and eventually succeeded. First, he found a young blonde to marry. She had the right background and her family had lots of money. Tony was terrified that she would find out about his family background and flimsy financial underpinnings, so he invited no one from his side of the family to the wedding.

Although not a very strong attorney, Tony was able to get his father-in-law to introduce him to his rich and influential friends during the golf matches that Tony played religiously. As his clientele grew, he earned more and more money, and he lived in one of the nicest areas of town. He also represented some of the area's most prestigious families. So Tony's ideal picture for himself was complete.

To this day, Tony goes out of his way to avoid anyone remotely associated with his past. At social situations, when he spots one of his associates from college who knows his background, he leaves the party or brushes off the old acquaintance by saying he doesn't remember him.

However, Tony confided in me a couple of years ago that he sometimes wakes up at night in a cold sweat. He has a recurring nightmare that his wife, father-in-law, and two of his biggest clients suddenly appear in the kitchen of his uncle's restaurant, where Tony is seated, stuffing tamales in his mouth while his aunt looks on. His wife starts screaming at him, "Who the hell are you, Tony?" Then Tony throws up the tamales all over his clients. Then, he says, he wakes up. He says he's been having this dream for about five years and is really getting sick of it. **$**

The Social Climber Game: Seeking Status

The Social Climber Game is status based. We seek status through this game because we think it offers us opportunities we otherwise wouldn't have. It's a combination of ego-based needs coupled with belonging needs. We want to belong and we want to do so as part of the wealthy set. We buy into the belief that if we can infiltrate the circles of the rich, we will eventually reap financial and social rewards.

And sometimes this works. There are hundreds of young men and women who have forged their wealth by networking, having superior talents or products, and working very smartly to get ahead. Larry Ellison of Oracle and Anita Roddick of the Body Shop are examples that come to mind. While individuals like these have played the Money Game, they typically haven't scammed how to get there, hiding their past. Many of them, in fact, have used it. They've leveraged who they are. They are very real about how they got where they are, owning their origins and often capitalizing on their backgrounds.

If we mask who we are and stoop to manipulate the wealthy to get their goodwill, we become master users. We tell the rich what we think they want to hear. We do things that may feel uncomfortable. We get used in order to use. We sell ourselves out for the possibility of wealth and success.

The Belief

For serious players of the Social Climber Game, money and wealth become an emotional life jacket. These players believe wealth will rescue them from an undesirable past and deliver them to a rosy new future. They seek validation for what they believe they're missing. If they can cozy up to wealth, they'll get warmed by the white-hot cash. Rubbing elbows with the rich can make them acceptable in society. It will make up for any and all deficits because people "forgive so much if you have more money than they do."

It's one thing to desire wealth and power. It's another to mask who and what we are to get it. When we hide our heritage and morph ourselves into a fiction, we're split into a duality that is difficult to keep up over time. Living a half-truth can be exhausting, as Tony was discovering. Only half of him was showing up in his life, while the other half was kept under wraps. As in the tale of Dorian Gray, who swapped eternal youth by keeping his aging persona locked in a putrid portrait in the attic, Tony's other self was languishing in the attic, buried under a heap of shame and resentment.

Tony believed he simply wasn't good enough. He was only good by association. Social climbers like Tony attach themselves to others; they have no faith in what they themselves have to offer. They seek power by reference. Like a symbiotic fungus, which survives at the mercy of the host, the Social Climber becomes the ultimate sycophant to the rich.

The Secret

By attempting to hide who they really are, Social Climbers breed feelings of deceit, shame, and guilt. The greatest loss for a social manipulator is the loss of integrity. Sometimes manipulators can't tell whom they resent more: themselves or their hosts.

They are haunted by the fear of being exposed. No matter how much status and wealth they acquire, they are always covering up something. They live in a state of hyperalertness. This can be emotionally and mentally exhausting. Having or not having money becomes only a minor aspect of this game. Being naked and rejected is the ultimate fear.

Game Triggers

The ultimate trigger of this game is shame. Players learn to be ashamed of who they are and where they came from. They have to make excuses for themselves. They must take on a new persona to escape the shame that pervades their self-image. Triggers can include:

- Coming from a minority heritage and growing up being ridiculed
- Knowing the sting of abject poverty
- Growing up with ego-based parents who live out their money fantasies through their children
- Facing rejection from the wealthy because you are too ill-bred to have money

- Suddenly finding wealth in your family through a marriage
- Getting rejected by financial institutions because of one's heritage, background, or lack of connections
- Getting sexually rejected due to one's background or lack of wealth

Disarming Strategies

Untangling from this shame-based game can be tough. Social manipulation is often a lifetime game because the rewards so often outweigh the pain. Getting ahead, having cash in the bank, getting bigger houses and more luxurious cars help salve childhood shame. A few spoons of caviar go a long way toward quelling a guilty conscience.

Typically, a player won't want to relinquish this game until he or she experiences some pain. For Tony, he was beginning to come unglued from having to remember everything he "had become" and disguising what he "was not supposed to be." Standing outside your own skin can work for a long time—at least until something like ill health, losing wealth, getting confronted, or getting exposed in an ugly way forces a look at how you've been operating.

If and when you are ready to begin recovery from the Social Climber Game, these ideas may be helpful:

- Write one page (no more than 100 words) about who you really are.
- While holding up a picture next to your face, look in the mirror to see who you were before you started to play the Social Climber Game. Now jot down three things you like about the real you and three you don't like about what you have become.
- Move slowly. It takes time to trust and get to know yourself again. Start to associate with people who knew you before you started the Social Climber Game. They will remember you as you were before.

Your New Way of Thinking

"By being who I am, and through the right use of money, I will attract the money I need."

Your Action Plan

Inner steps to take:

1. Reflect on the traits and qualities of the real you that you miss. Remember, valuing money more than your own identity will lead to future troubles that are much greater than the currently perceived financial problems you may be in.

2. Fold a piece of paper in half vertically and create two lists of your qualities: "What My Social Status Says I Am" and "What I Am." In the "What My Social Status Says I Am" column, list your possessions, clubs, offices, honors, and awards. In the "What I Am" column, list your personal traits (such as loving, skilled, focused, committed, goal-directed, compassionate). Now asterisk the items in both lists that you emphasize most in your relationships. Consider how much of "What I Am" you are sharing in your relationships.

3. Now try this: Take another piece of paper, fold it in half vertically, and create lists of two other qualities: "What My Friends and Acquaintances Think I Offer" and "What I Think I Am." In the first column list the stuff of your social status (possessions, memberships, offices, awards, and so on). In the second column, list your personal traits (loving, skilled, focused, committed, goal-directed, compassionate) that you value in yourself. Then asterisk the items in either list that you think your friends and acquaintances put the most emphasis on in your relationships. Compare your two sets of lists and consider how real your relationships are and how you want them to be in the future.

4. Write a paragraph about who you are without your social status. If it's a short paragraph, get to work expanding

yourself as a balanced human being and broaden your interests.

5. Tell everyone, "I'm a Social Climber, and that's how I seek to get ahead." Such candor may disarm your friends and allow you to be more honest.

6. Find a new money mantra. Say instead, "I will be me. And my satisfaction will come from living contentedly with neither too much nor too little."

7. Write your eulogy as you think your children might write it, using at least 100 words. Consider if this is the legacy you want to leave.

8. Create a list of the most important experiences you have had in your life and see how many relate to social status. Then create a list of the most important experiences you want to have in your life. How many revolve around social status? If you concentrated on the nonstatus ones, how would your life change? Do you want it to change in that manner?

Financial steps to take:

1. Write out how much money you think you really need to obtain life's necessities. Then don't put any energy into getting more than that.

2. Surround yourself with people who can't be of social or financial help to you. Volunteer in a soup kitchen, for example, or work in the ghetto or barrio.

3. Visit a sick or dying friend, acquaintance, or relative. Ask him or her about what has had meaning in his or her life.

Think about It

"Too many people spend money they haven't earned, to buy things they don't want, to impress people they don't like."

—Will Rogers

THE SOCIAL CLIMBER GAME

Rules	If I hang out with the rich, I'll end up rich.
Belief	I can acquire worth and self-esteem if I rub elbows with the rich.
Secret	If they knew who I am and how little I really have, they'd reject me. I hate myself that I'm not more. I hate them because I have to do so much to be accepted.
Feeling	Inferiority, self-loathing, resentment
Game Triggers	Being rejected, being judged for being poor or in minority, needing validation
Disarming Strategies	Consider who you are in and of your own talents, abilities, and self-worth.
Persona	Manipulator
Action	Check your motives, get to know yourself, learn to value yourself for who you are rather than who you know.

Chapter Eleven

Game #9: The Self-Worth Game

Eric's Story

Eric grew up working on weekends and during summers in his dad's landscaping business. Eric and his dad were very close, working side by side designing landscapes, doing yard upkeep, and installing irrigation systems.

Then Eric went to college to study architecture. He only occasionally worked with his father over the next several years, and his father's business leveled off, with no significant gains. After Eric graduated from a local college, he was floundering, trying to decide on an occupation. He enjoyed partying with his friends and seemed directionless. His dad then asked him to help him run his business. Eric thought about it for a while, then jumped at the idea of earning some decent money, learning how to manage his dad's workers, and putting his architectural skills to work.

The first two years, Eric thrived. He said that working with his dad gave him purpose, a direction, and he also liked seeing his design work come to life in gardens and water fountains. Eric loved the combination of using both his hands and his mind. He felt invigorated by being creative and getting out in the dirt

planting, digging, and directing other men on how best to imple-
ment his ideas.

Eric started to push his dad toward bigger, riskier projects. His
dad usually turned down these high-exposure ventures. He was afraid
to take risks with his business. He said he was comfortable with the
customers he had now and he didn't want to risk that stability.

Eric became frustrated. Increasingly, Eric and his dad argued.
Eric wanted to exert his authority and control over more of the
company. His dad criticized Eric for "being too big for your
britches." He said what he had always done with his customers had
worked for him and he had no intention of changing.

Finally, Eric had had enough. He told his dad he was out: "I am
going to start my own company and do all the things you are too old
and bullheaded to do." Eric's father screamed back at him, "You
ungrateful brat. You go right ahead. You'll be sorry you left me."

Despite his father's warning, Eric's company did well. Because
both companies were working with high net-worth estates, however, they began to compete in bidding for new customers. Soon
Eric's risk-taking paid off, and he won a reputation for innovative
ideas and quick solutions. His father, on the other hand, began to
have difficulty finding new customers. He had to lay off a couple of
his employees.

For a time, Eric gloated. He felt vindicated. His pride grew, and
he gloried in having "beaten" his dad. Then, one Christmas, something happened. By now, Eric had a lovely wife and three children,
aged two, four, and five. They hadn't seen their grandparents in
three years, though, because Eric and his father still weren't talking.
Late in the morning, little Eric, Jr., came to his father carrying his
brand-new red dump truck. He got up in Eric's lap, looked up into
his face, and asked, "Did Grandpa ever give you a big red dump
truck like this one?"

Eric felt a stab in his heart. He thought of Christmases when he
was a boy. He remembered how his dad had shown him how to
move dirt and twigs around to make a corral for his toy ponies. He
remembered how he thought his dad was the smartest man in the
world that day.

Sitting there, with his son on his lap, Eric was overcome with sadness. He realized how much he missed his dad. He put little Eric down and went to his study for a while. When he returned for Christmas dinner a little later, his wife noticed his eyes were red.

Later that night, Eric couldn't sleep. He realized that his ego was cutting him off from his father, that his need to be right was poisoning the entire family. He began to feel ashamed for wanting to show how he could best his dad. He was afraid he had gone too far and that he would cause his dad's business to go under. Finally, he realized how much he missed his old man. He missed how close they'd been and how much he wanted to share his failures—and his successes—with him.

When Eric returned to work after the holidays, he vowed not to take any more business from his dad. In fact, he approached his dad and admitted, "I am an ass sometimes." His father laughed and said, "Well, I guess you had a good role model." They hugged for the first time in four years.

Father and son started working on some joint projects. They built a renewed, more trusting relationship. Eric thanked God that his son had helped him realize that his relationship with his dad was more important than any Money Game. $

The Self-Worth Game: Proving Ourselves

Sometimes we play the Self-Worth Game out of a need to prove ourselves. Money becomes a vital yardstick to tell us how we are valued. Often this plays itself out in games to "make more than Mom or Dad made."

Our financial lingo is rich with measurement terms: "Net worth," "capital gains," "profits and losses," "debits and credits," "pluses and minuses." With money, we infer we have value. Without it, we suspect we are a deficit.

Many men are always trying to "make the grade," for example, if they've felt put down by their fathers. They recall moments when they were embarrassed by Dad or felt he used his authority to undermine them. Many women experience this competition with either Mom or Dad as a challenge to "marry up" or have a bigger house or more children or more wealth or a better career.

Maybe for either gender, when our parents feel inadequate, they often project that inadequacy onto us. We grow up behind the curve and are determined to catch up. One way we do that is by making money as a way to get even with various authority figures. If Dad gets a Mercedes, we get a Lexus. If our boss buys a six-bedroom house, we do everything we can to get one with eight. Robin's story is a case in point.

Robin's Story

A stockbroker, Robin joined a Southern California brokerage after having grown up in a big city on the East Coast. He was driven by the need to avoid financial failure, which had humbled his father. Robin, seeing his father's fate as an embarrassment, made an early decision not to suffer the same humiliation, no matter what it took.

When Robin was a boy, he often got beaten up by bigger boys in school. That was partly because Robin was part of a minority group, and others made fun of him because his father was the school's janitor. Robin tried to hide this, but everyone knew about his father anyway. Robin learned to stick close to his neighborhood most of the time so he wouldn't get picked on.

Once, however, when he was ten years old, Robin's mother sent him to the market a few blocks away to get some milk. His face still goes white when he tells about being in the rear of the store near the icebox that held the milk, when suddenly two young gunmen burst through the door and lunged at the old man behind the cash register. Robin froze. "I knew that if they saw me, I would be dead. I felt completely helpless. I scooted around behind the stacks of egg cartons. The robbers took their money, and then I heard the shot. They'd popped the old man in the head. I stayed down behind the eggs for what seemed like hours. I was there when the cops found me, behind the eggs, standing in my own urine. I'd peed in my pants.

"Now, I curse that day. I curse that my father made us live in that terrible neighborhood. I never forgave him for not protecting me from that horrible place. I curse that he was only a janitor, that he never tried harder to be anything else. That night, I prayed to God to get me out of there. I made a pact with God that night that I would make enough money to get out of that neighborhood and away from my old man, and never look back."

Robin says he gritted his teeth and lived through years of continuous teasing after that. He says he only had a couple of pairs of pants to wear to school. He only had new shoes every two years or so. The rich boys loved to harass him. He got his first job at eleven selling newspapers. He'd always worked since that day. He began to use his money to buy his own clothes. When he was sixteen, he'd bought his own used car. By seventeen he was gone for good.

Robin worked his way through high school and junior college, earning a scholarship to a reputable university. He graduated in the top 5 percent of his business-school class. He never invited his parents to any of his graduations. He rarely returned their calls and letters.

Robin was completely focused on finding the most lucrative career he could. He figured he could make the fastest money as a stockbroker. He liked the feel and smell of money. He liked money that moved fast. And he liked to trade with big accounts. He funneled all of his effort, day and night, into his work. He marked up bonds to clients at higher-than-normal commissions. He also made a regular practice of buying bonds that his clients were selling at a bigger-than-normal discount, and then repurchasing these bargain bonds for his own account.

Robin was absolutely determined to win every annual award. He would stop at nothing to make a deal. One day he was so desperate to qualify for the year-end club that he went to see one of his most lucrative clients. Fred was an eighty-year-old retired television store owner and was dying of prostate cancer. Robin needed to make one more transaction to hit his year-end target, and he thought Fred would roll over if Robin advised him to invest in a certain cable-television limited partnership. When Robin arrived at the old man's home, however, he found a nurse bent over Fred, who was lying in a near-coma.

Robin couldn't rouse Fred to sign the paperwork, so he took a desperate step. He called a local buddy of his from college who had become a doctor. He asked the friend to come over and give Fred a shot of adrenaline so Robin could prop Fred up and get him to sign the paperwork. Reluctantly, Robin's friend complied, and they finally got Fred to hold the pen so that Robin could smear Fred's signature across the bottom of the page. A short while later, Robin and his friend left. Fred slipped into a coma and died later that evening.

Robin amassed more money in the first two years in the business than his father had made in his life. Robin's father died when Robin was thirty. He went alone to the funeral. When he returned, he set a new goal for himself: make $2 million by age thirty-five.

Robin lived alone. His apartment looked like a satellite brokerage firm. Financial magazines and newspapers littered every room, including the bathroom. He kept the financial cable channel running twenty-four hours a day so he could have up-to-the-minute info. He rarely dated because most women's eyes glazed over after two or three hours of constant money patter. They told him he was a bore.

After he made his $2 million goal, he seemed to wind down for a time. He told me he had this really empty feeling in the pit of his stomach. Sometimes he would just stare out the window for a half hour and ignore the numbers moving on the Big Board. After a few weeks, he figured he'd set a new goal for himself: make $3 million by age forty. But he still pretty much lived a lonely life, and spent his off time talking to financial cronies at the yacht club on weekends.

One Sunday, he met Terri, whose father owned a local company that rented yachts for the day. Terri was a pretty down-to-earth girl. She was thirty, had a degree in education, and loved to sail. On weekends, she taught kids and adults the basics of sailing. Robin decided to take some lessons.

Within a few months, they were dating seriously. By fall, they were married. By the time Robin was forty, he'd made his $3 million goal, but he was devoting less and less time to the financials. He and Terri were busy raising two great children. Whenever Robin got so obsessed that she'd find him littering even the bathroom with the financial papers, she'd yell, "Robin, get your head out of that newspaper and get a life. Let's go sailing." Their mutual love of sailing, and their great kids, helped transform Robin, and he began to find some balance in his life.

One day when the children were nine and eleven, he sat down and told them the story of the robbers back in that ratty neighborhood where he grew up. He told his boy and girl that he'd made a terrible decision that day. "I want to tell you that your dad has made some big mistakes. I hated my father for a long time because I thought he'd shafted me. I decided to blame my dad for my problems. I couldn't accept him for what he was and I had to be better. I was a really bitter, self-centered person until I met your mom and had you two." He admitted to them that his bitterness had helped him make a lot of money. "But," he told them, "all the money in the world can't match what it's like to be your dad. I hope you can forgive me for being so awful to your grandpa. I want to be a better person to you both. I hope you'll let me." $

The Belief

For both Eric and Robin, the driving belief behind their Money Game was that money was a way out. It was a ticket out of their past, away from their heritage, out from under parental pressure. They believed that money and success would give them the edge over circumstances that were keeping them down. Theirs was a do-or-die game. Money offered freedom from perceived limitations. Both men did whatever they could to distance themselves from past influences and carve out their own niche.

The belief is that money offers us a way out, but it also gives us a way to become someone else. We believe that money will give us stature, and to some degree it does. At work, we are constantly reminded that money is stature. As employees we are rewarded for completing work that will add to our employer's bottom line. We learn to jump through hoops for greater pay, which reinforces the belief of our self-worth as net worth. Further, if a company (or really, our commercial and economic system) gets us to believe that money is the answer to our life problems, then we are hooked.

This is how many of us find ourselves as slaves to our employers. Without our jobs and our pay, we would conceivably have no value. This myth gets etched deeply in our subconscious, particularly for men, for whom it is chronically reinforced by society that their self-worth is wrapped up in their jobs and earning power. We aren't even aware of the degree to which we are conditioned to attain monetary rewards so that we can have a positive self-worth.

The Secret

The deep, dark secret of this game is a deep-seated lack of confidence, and, in some cases, feelings of personal failure or even loathing of ourselves or others. It's a learned rejection of self that often gets projected outward onto others. We feel driven to distance ourselves from influencers or authority figures whom we think have harmed us or who don't hold us in esteem. In the process, we begin to disown parts of ourselves.

This game goes beyond mere growing up, leaving home, and establishing our own identity. It becomes a competitive game where we sometimes devalue the good we've come from, and embrace the powers of a money-and-success society to help us rise like a phoenix to a new social persona. Money and success become the vehicles to another life.

The problem is, we end up disowning some of our heritage and natural abilities. We may become resentful or bitter if we didn't learn the values from our parents that will make us loved and rewarded in adult society. When money takes us out of our bitterness or self-doubt, even temporarily, we think money is what makes us happy. Money gives us the endorsement we crave, so we embrace it like a surrogate parent or a new religion. We disown our origins and natural instincts because they appear to have nothing to do with our new selves.

The deception, of course, is that we do bring those skills, talents, and also resiliencies from our childhood experiences. They are part of what has fueled our power today. If we disown those parts of ourselves, we are using half of our power. We keep one hand tied behind our back and wonder why we feel disabled.

Game Triggers

Both natural and unnatural events and circumstances can trigger this game. Some are:

- Getting rejected by a parent and being forced to leave home
- Being abused or abandoned by a parent
- Feeling ashamed of one's heritage
- Growing up with poverty and ridicule
- Getting reinforced for work performance
- Watching society denigrate people (particularly men) who are unsuccessful monetarily in life
- Observing influencers value someone for bottom-line money success versus contribution to society

Disarming Strategies

As Edgar Z. Friedenberg said in *The Vanishing Adolescent*, "What we must decide is perhaps how we are valuable rather than how valuable we are." We need to discover how we contribute and are valued as separate from our capacity to earn. Some of the ways to do this are:

- Define who you are by listing where you started out in life and how far you have progressed. Realize you are not what you have materially generated.

- Make a list of what you learned from your parents and your heritage. Then asterisk how many of them you have used to help make you a success today.
- When you find yourself in a situation in which you may elect to play the Self-Worth Game, picture yourself as a child and ask him or her how he or she would feel about the action you are about to take. Then proceed with what you believe to now be in your best interest.

Your New Way of Thinking

"There isn't enough money in the world to get me to be what I'm not, to say what I don't believe in, or to live my life by other than the blueprint of my soul. To alter who I am is not only a travesty to myself, but more importantly it is cheating the world out of the most important gifts I have to offer."

Your Action Plan

Inner steps to take:

1. Have an intergenerational talk. If there are concerns about how parents or children regard the relationship, don't let them get in the way. Talk about those issues.
2. Accept yourself for who you are. Don't measure yourself by other people's definition of what your worth should be. Success is defined from the inside of ourselves, not by what others say or do. It is up to you to define what you are about and what makes you a success.
3. Fold a piece of paper in half vertically and create two lists of your qualities: "What I Offer" and "What I Am." In the "What I Offer" column, list your stuff (bank accounts, houses, cars, and so on). In the "What I Am" column, list your personal traits (such as loving, skilled, focused, committed, goal-directed, compassionate). Now asterisk the

items in both lists that you emphasize most in your relationships. Consider how much of "What I Am" you are sharing in your relationships.

4. Now try this: Take another piece of paper, fold it in half vertically, and create lists of two other qualities: "What My Friends and Acquaintances Think I Offer" and "What I Think I Am." In the first column, list the stuff (possessions, social status, and so on) for which you think your friends and acquaintances value you. In the second column, list your personal traits (loving, skilled, focused, committed, goal-directed, compassionate) for which you think you should be valued. Then asterisk the items in either list that you think you put the most emphasis on in your relationships. Compare your two sets of lists and consider how real your relationships are and how you want them to be in the future.

5. Get a friend or associate to also make a list: "What I Value You For."

6. Find a new money mantra. Say instead, "I will be myself and share with the world who I really am."

7. Write a paragraph about who you are without your money. If it's a short paragraph, get to work expanding yourself as a balanced human being and broaden your interests.

Financial steps to take:

1. Educate your children now about money. Set up a savings account with them. Do some fun things together each week that revolve around money lessons you want to teach them. Help them learn to use money as a resource, not as a definer of their individual worth. Check out the Web site for the Jump$tart Coalition for Personal Financial Literacy (*www.jumpstart.org*). It's filled with ideas about how to teach kids about money and its uses.

2. Draw up a list of life goals and estimate how much money it will take to accomplish them. Then develop a practical plan to achieve them. Much self-doubt comes from not

having such a plan in place and believing that one's goals are beyond reach.

Think about It

"If money be not thy servant, it will be thy master. The covetous cannot so properly be said to possess wealth, as that it may be said to possess him."

—Francis Bacon

THE SELF-WORTH GAME	
Rules	I am my money. My money makes me who I am.
Belief	With money, I am somebody.
Secret	Without my money, I may not have much to offer.
Feeling	Anger, resentment, worthlessness
Game Triggers	Desperation triggered by not having money and status
Disarming Strategies	Explore your value as separate from your money.
Persona	House of Cards
Action	Build self-esteem based on all your values, not just your net worth.

Self-Worth Assessment

After the following statements, write *T* for those that are true for you, and *F* for those that are false.

1. I feel better about myself the more money I make. _____
2. I give up my power to those with more money. _____
3. My parents gave me the message that they value me more the more money I have earned. _____
4. The income level of people I know sometimes affects how much I respect them. _____
5. Being unemployed for a short time would make me feel bad about myself. _____

6. I feel more comfortable around those with the same, or less, money as me. _____

7. I am careful about whom I share my finances with. _____

8. I have relatives, parents, loved ones, or friends who sometimes look down at me due to my lack of money. _____

9. At the end of the year, if I haven't gotten ahead financially I consider myself a loser. _____

10. I sometimes think of myself as stupid, dumb, or slow with money matters. _____

11. I sometimes feel I have to live up to someone else's financial or success expectations of me. _____

12. I find myself competing with my parents regarding who makes the most money and has the most stuff. _____

13. When I hit a bumpy money period, I find myself feeling disgusted about myself. _____

14. I was sometimes judged as a child based on how much money or toys I had and I was hurt by it. _____

15. I worry about money every day. _____

If you answered more than six of these as true, you may be playing a Self-Worth Game.

Chapter Twelve

Game #10: The Kiddo Game

Tim's Story

Tim was a successful accountant who worked for one of the larger accounting firms. Although he worked hard and earned decent money, he was never made a partner.

Tim married Julie, who came from a middle-class family that lived as though it was upper class. Thus, Julie had top-drawer tastes and would request that she and Tim stay at the finest hotels, eat at the best restaurants, and wear the nicest clothes. Although Tim was uneasy about this, he went along with it because he believed he would soon make partner. Tim and Julie eventually found that they were overspending to live the life they thought they deserved. They had to resort to using their credit cards to live a high lifestyle. Later, they had to take out an equity line of credit on their house in order to keep up appearances. When Tim felt insecure about money issues, he would turn to his wife and say, "Well, I guess your family will always bail us out if my income doesn't cover us."

Later, Tim lost his job after not making partner and being with the firm for fifteen years. Julie had to go to work. The couple cut back at first, but once Julie was employed, they went back to spending money as if it were going out of style. When they were pinched, Julie's parents would give them annual handouts to supplement their lifestyle. By middle age, Tim and Julie had five children and had seen Julie's parents' estate rise to over $1 million. They knew that Julie would inherit all of this, so they just let the bills mount.

Suddenly, the stock market contracted for a few years. Julie saw her cut of the inheritance decline to $300,000 before taxes. Knowing this did not seem to bother Tim or Julie too much; they continued to take two-week vacations at Disney World and other destinations. Both drove expensive cars and lived the life to which they thought they were entitled.

Finally, Tim and Julie reached the end of their financial rope. They had no more credit cards to use, and they had loans on everything. They were drowning in debt. Julie's dad was still alive (although her mother had passed on), so she couldn't get her inheritance yet. The only thing left for the couple to do was to file for bankruptcy. They lost their house, their cars, any trust fund money for their children, and their art collection.

Julie's dad had them sign a note from her future inheritance, and then advanced them enough money for the family to live in a modest condominium. Now fifty, Tim worked as a mid-level accountant, and Julie kept a day-care center to make ends meet. **$**

The Kiddo Game: Mommy and Daddy Will Provide

The Kiddo Game is easy to fall into if you have had parents or family who have always supported you financially. In essence, you never grow up. You can be fifty and still be getting an "allowance."

Unfortunately, we learn this game at our parents' knees. They've helped create a codependency relationship that makes us dependent on them for financial support. There are always two players in the Kiddo Game: the money provider and the money user. If we are playing this game, we have literally been reinforced not to stop playing it. We have been kept in a childlike money state. Therefore, we haven't learned adult skills around money. Usually, without some sort of major wakeup call, we have very little motivation to stop playing the game. And, typically, the money provider is quite satisfied to keep us tied to his or her apron strings. It's a pernicious game of use and be used. Of course, it's a one-up, one-down game, but the difference is that it's coated in family dynamics.

The Belief

When we play the Kiddo Game, we entertain a belief that Mom and Dad, or their estate, will perpetually fund us and/or rescue us from financial predicaments. We typically learn very little about managing money because we don't need to know anything. We remain financially ignorant. On the needs hierarchy, we remain at the physiological and belonging needs, because Mom and Dad are providing and we need to belong to get the financial support.

People playing the Kiddo Game may continue to play the game even if their endless money pot comes into doubt. Like Tim and Julie, we may operate under the illusion of perpetual wealth and run up large debts and acquire financial baggage. Many American families operate under this belief system, especially because Baby Boomer statistics support the myth. When Baby Boomers' parents die and transfer their wealth to their children, it will be the largest wealth transfer in the history of our country.

Another version of the Kiddo Game is played if we believe our tax return or year-end bonus will bail us out of current financial predicaments. We again demonstrate a naiveté with regard to money if we pin our financial hopes on an outside windfall to rescue us. Peter and Matilda's story is a case in point.

Peter and Matilda's Story

Peter and Matilda grew up in a lower-middle-class neighborhood. Peter had a shoe repair business, and Matilda raised their children at home. They had a very wealthy relative, Peter's uncle, who had served as a U.S. diplomatic representative in embassies throughout the world. Peter and Matilda were always told by Peter's uncle and aunt, "We will take care of you in our will."

Peter and his family religiously spent Sunday afternoons and Wednesday evenings driving the twenty miles to the uncle and aunt's house to see them. As Peter's uncle and aunt got older, they continued to discuss their wealth with Peter and Matilda and how the couple "would be taken care of upon our death." Peter and Matilda's children hated going to see the elderly relatives because they lived in a townhome without a yard. The home also had so many breakables and precious heirlooms that the children were always being cautioned, "Don't break anything here or you will be in big trouble."

When Peter's uncle passed away, Peter and Matilda became even more dutiful and stepped up seeing the aunt, visiting an additional day each week. After twenty long years, the aunt also died. Peter and Matilda thought that their money problems would be over.

But to their surprise, they inherited nothing. When the will was read, the money was split among the eleven grandchildren. Peter and Matilda, as parents of two of the grandchildren, got nothing. Peter became incensed. He demanded his two teenage children each give half of their inherited money to Peter and Matilda. The children refused, setting it aside in money-market accounts for their college educations.

Peter and Matilda remained irate. They forced their son and daughter both to leave home at eighteen, and the children are still estranged from their parents, despite now having families of their own. $

The Secret

Manipulating to get what we think "is due us" is at the heart of the Kiddo Game. This is a family quid pro quo game. We give love to get cash; we give cash to get love back. Money becomes a substitute for the natural love and trust that should bind adults. The money becomes a substitute, a stand-in for true love, trust, and intimacy. Thus, the manufactured relationships can come apart when funds are withheld or withdrawn.

The most debilitating part of the Kiddo Game is that the dynamic is equivalent to incest. Unlike sexual incest, this is family money incest. As distasteful as this may sound, parents (or uncles or aunts or grandparents) pay their children to curry emotional favor. Children give love and affection based on being paid and rewarded. The elders prostitute their children. The children learn to be prostitutes. When the dynamic stops for some reason, the children, even as adults, react as stunted children, which, of course, they are because they have learned no financial independence as a result of being habitually abused.

Parents who abuse their children financially sacrifice their children for themselves. They don't teach their offspring healthy behaviors with money. They can't set healthy boundaries with their children because doing so would help teach their children independence, a dynamic a dependent parent can't tolerate. Their money is their power. Typically, the parents themselves have been victims of financial incest. They know nothing more than to perpetuate the behavior.

Children who find out as adults that they have been "raped and manipulated with money" undergo a process similar to sexual-incest recovery victims. They feel betrayed. They feel victimized. They feel used and abused. They doubt their own worth. They have corrupted ego systems. And often they tap into the intense hatred and betrayal toward parental figures who used them in this way. They may begin to realize that their parents were so dysfunctional that they had to cannibalize their children basically to feel satiated themselves. This can be a gut-wrenching realization.

Their emotional growth and maturity has been manipulated and abused by parents or family figures who need to manipulate a weaker family member to get their needs met. Money incest becomes a vicious cycle where money buys love and loyalty at the expense of honest trust.

Unfortunately, when parents teach their children this game, the children often then repeat the dynamic with their own children and partners. The dynamic is self-perpetuating, unless an intervention such as a death, a bankruptcy, or a life-threatening illness disrupts the pattern.

Game Triggers

This game is typically passed down through a family, generation by generation. It is a learned dependency in which both parent and child are in a vicious codependency cycle. The game is triggered when a child is born into a money-incestuous family. Other circumstances or life events that can trigger the Kiddo Game include:

- When parents receive an inheritance and contemplate where and how the money will be spent
- When financially codependent teens or young adults get their first credit cards
- When Mom and Dad continually bail their kids out of financially irresponsible situations
- When children are rewarded for groveling, pleading, and rolling over so they can obtain money
- When a child knows he or she will acquire a large sum of money at eighteen or twenty-one years of age due to a Uniform Gift to Minors Account or a trust coming due, thereby taking away the child's incentive to work or make his or her own way in life

Disarming Strategies

To disarm from this game takes courage. Consider some of the following to disengage from the game:

First, ask yourself: "Could I survive for three months without financial help from my family? Six months? One year?" If you answered no to the any of the questions, admit that you have a degree of codependency on financial support.

Second, make a list of the areas in which you feel financially dependent. These might include:

- Credit card debt over $2,000
- Down payment on a house made to you by family members whom you have yet to pay back
- College tuition your parents are paying for your college-age children
- House or car payments being made by family members
- Cars or homes you are using at no cost because a family member loaned them to you
- Loans made to you by employers or partners that make you dependent on the ongoing relationships
- Any commitment you have made to a family member that requires you to do something in exchange for real estate, trust fund money, cars, homes, or cash

Another step is to evaluate your confidence about your financial skills. On a scale of 1 to 5, with 5 being very knowledgeable, rate yourself on the following areas of financial knowledge and acumen:

Checking account maintenance _____

Savings account maintenance _____

Debt payment and scheduling _____

Budgeting _____

Real estate investment _____

Basic investment (money-market accounts, CDs, etc.) _____

Basic financial planning _____

Mid-level investment (stocks, bonds, etc.) _____

Basic retirement planning _____

High-level investment (futures, options, commodities, etc.) _____

Commercial investment _____

Next, have both a family member and an independent, financially savvy individual rate you on the same areas. Compare your scores and notice how accurate your self-perception is, compared to the views of others.

Finally, disarming the game means taking a hard look at what you know and how many quid pro quo financial arrangements exist in your life. Consult with a fee-based financial advisor to get an objective picture of how independent you are financially. Have your advisor rate you on your dependence or independence, then follow the Action Plan below.

Your New Way of Thinking

"I willingly choose to be responsible with my money and live within my means."

Your Action Plan

Inner steps to take:

1. Assess your financial acumen using the assessment at the end of the chapter. If you score poorly, resolve to take serious steps to increase your financial independence over the next year.
2. Disengage from unhealthy relationships in your family. This means saying no when money carrots are dangled in front of you. This also means going to a bank or credit union for financial help instead of to the bank of Mom/Dad.
3. Give up your victim persona. Process your childhood pain with money by working with a therapist and start building a responsible money future. Aim to move past your family drama with money and to refocus your profound capacity to feel victimized into compassion, love, and understanding for others—perhaps other family money victims. Use your learning to help others.

4. Use your natural anger at what you have allowed to happen to get you motivated to put an end to this manipulative behavior and get on with a productive life.

Financial steps to take:

1. Come up with a financial agreement with family members to pay off debts, loans, and assets with interest in a pre-scribed amount of time. Turn the family arrangement into a financial arrangement and treat your relationships like financial ones, with penalties for nonperformance.

2. Get rid of or consolidate any debt you have amassed under the illusion of paying "when your ship comes in."

3. Get a financial consultant instead of a relative to help you reorganize your finances in an adult way.

4. Educate yourself by taking general investment or money management courses at a community college.

5. Gently confront relatives when they try to use money to win your goodwill. Your newfound independence will help them get healthy as well.

Think about It

"It is not the man who has too little who is poor, but the one who hankers after more. . . . You ask what is the proper limit to a person's wealth? First having what is essential, and second, having what is enough."

—Seneca

THE KIDDO GAME	
Rules	I get money for love. I give money to show love.
Belief	I don't have to take charge of my money responsibilities because Mom and Dad will bail me out.
Secret	You give me money, I give you love. I give you money, you give me loyalty and unconditional regard. We manipulate each other and that's the way it's always been.
Feeling	Dependent, afraid, manipulated
Game Triggers	Being born in a Kiddo Game family, handling money
Disarming Strategies	Acknowledge and take responsibility for your money dependency. Commit to stopping the cycle of money abuse.
Persona	Marionette
Action	Take charge of your financial life. Set appropriate financial boundaries and teach the same thing to your children.

Financial Acumen Assessment

After the following statements, write *T* for those that are true for you, and *F* for those that are false.

1. I know right now what my net worth is. ____
2. I have clear financial goals that I re-evaluate each year. ____
3. I have a budget that I follow and update regularly. ____
4. I pretty much pay my bills early or on time and get rid of debt as soon as I can. ____
5. I actively participate in managing my investments and savings. ____
6. I have at least six months' savings in the bank for emergencies. ____
7. I actively save at least 5 percent of my income per year. ____
8. I balance my checkbook regularly. ____
9. I don't withdraw money from my retirement accounts even when things get a little difficult. ____
10. I pay my income taxes on time and without remorse. ____
11. If I had to, I could live on my existing resources for at least two years. ____

12. I know exactly how much I spend, how much I save, and how much I need to live. ____

13. I understand my investments and am well versed on the risks I have taken. ____

14. I have my will or trust agreement updated every three years. ____

15. My liabilities/payments don't exceed 50 percent of my income. ____

16. If I use someone to manage my assets, I detail the terms rather than the reverse. ____

17. I contribute enough to my retirement plan to get my employer's full matching contribution. ____

18. I keep up to date on changes occurring in the financial marketplace. ____

19. I have a professional money, tax, or investment advisor.
____

20. If I have a partner, we fully disclose all of our assets and discuss our life goals with money. ____

If you answered less than six of these as true, you need to up your financial acumen.

Chapter Thirteen

Game #11: The Mistrust Game

Ron's Story

Ron, in his mid-thirties, owned a nail-manufacturing business that he'd inherited from his dad. The firm had grown from tiny, East Los Angeles roots in the 1930s to a million-dollar company that now ran at 90 percent capacity, two shifts a day. This assured Ron and his sister of steady incomes for life without much work. However, Ron knew there was a lot more money to be made if he could figure out how to increase the plant's capacity. He often tinkered with the equipment to get it to run faster and better.

Ron was married to Clare, who had worked as a travel agent, making under $10 an hour, before they had children. Clare's father had died when she was three. Her mother had raised her on a meager salary from the telephone company where Clare's mother had worked for thirty years. Now Clare stayed at home, devoting her time and energy to raising their three children. Clare felt she deserved to buy the finer things in life because she had been deprived as a kid and because she spent so much time stuck at home with the kids. Besides, she reasoned, Ron's father had passed on now, and Ron and his sister had inherited the company. They were rich. Clare, therefore, acquired a taste for shopping. She could easily spend a month's worth of Ron's salary in one afternoon of shopping.

Ron felt tremendous pressure to make more money and take his business to the next level. He also was always trying to put the brakes on Clare's spending. At the same time, Ron was an avid golfer, and he took every vacation and many Saturdays and Sundays to play thirty-six holes a day.

In the office, Ron could often be heard on the phone lecturing Clare about how much she'd spent that month on clothes or house decorations. Other times, Clare would come steaming down to the plant with the youngest in tow. Though Ron slammed the glass door shut to get some privacy, he and Clare could be heard arguing even by those in the employee parking lot. He would yell at her for her department store bills. She would scream at him for his Golf Mart purchases and entertaining bills. They would blame each other for the tight money situation they felt they were in and the lack of college money they'd saved for the kids.

Despite the arguments and recriminations, the couple found clever ways around each other to satisfy their money addictions. Gradually, each had started money laundering over their ten-year marriage. That is, they each learned how to take money out of the family resources without the other knowing.

Clare figured out that she could always pad the grocery bill by taking cash back at the checkout stand. At first, she'd take out an extra $20 or $30. Later it became $50, $100, and $150. She'd use her "grocery cash" to get her nails and hair done or to buy special cosmetics or new dishes. At the end of the month, when Ron went over the bills, he just thought the grocery bill was pretty high. He didn't question it much, however, because, he said, "we have three boys and they eat a lot." Therefore, when Ron yelled at Clare about her spending, he was only looking at the $500 and $600 department-store purchases; he never even knew about the rest of her laundering.

Ron, on the other hand, had also figured out how to hide the money he spent from Clare. He had lots of business lunches with vendors, other business associates, as well as golfing buddies. Often he'd pay the bill with his credit card, then get his buddies to give him cash for their share of the bill. He'd then take his "expense cash" and buy the hottest new driver or putter or outfit his sports car with the newest speakers. As far as Clare knew, these were all business expenses, and she never realized how much Ron was sinking into his toys.

Ron also had a few assets with his sister that Clare didn't know about. Clare thought Ron had loaned his sister some money for her time-share business. In fact, Ron was part-owner of some of his sister's time-share condos around the world, and he pumped the money he made from the investments back into his business so Clare couldn't spend it and the company could grow.

Clare blamed Ron for not being able to get more money out of the business so "we can have the things we deserve." Ron blamed Clare for being "a spendthrift and not caring about the family or me." The couple reported to a money counselor that they both really loved each other and wanted their marriage to work. However, both were hoping the money counselor would help them find ways of making or getting more money so they wouldn't have to divulge their secrets to each other. $

The Mistrust Game: Money Secrets

The Mistrust Game is played by those who keep money secrets in order to conceal their spending. In a couple's relationship, however, this can have far-reaching repercussions. It's a game many of us learn early on.

The game is about maintaining control of what we believe is "my money." Sharing money, especially when we use money to get individual satisfaction, can become a life-or-death struggle over who gets supreme control. If a partner blocks our spending and we get our satisfaction, self-worth, or "high" out of that spending, we see the other partner as robbing us, somehow cutting off our lifeblood. When there's a high level of mistrust between partners or family members, we go to great lengths to maneuver for control. When the Mistrust Game is in full gear, it quickly spreads to every area of the couple's life. Struggles for control, either openly or covertly, develop rapidly.

Couples with relationship problems find money discussions especially difficult. Discussing money issues is the number-one tension producer reported by most couples, and money is also reportedly one of the chief causes of divorce in the United States.

According to couples' therapists, when those money problems are not put on the table and examined, they go underground and take on a life of their own. Then events can quickly escalate out of control, depending on how closed the couple's relationship is. Money mistrust may begin as soon as the honeymoon ends. Couples will often revert back to the ways their families operated with money, attempting to exert control by utilizing their own family's rules and behaviors. The threat posed by a mate's set of money beliefs, values, and attitudes is enough to scare many couples right out of their newly formed relationship. At best, a newly married couple will experience greater intensity in all areas of their lives where money is concerned.

Whether newlyweds or married long-term, some couples throw more money at the problem thinking that will solve the communication and trust issues. Others try to control one another's spending. Either way, there is a strong need to obscure money behavior and not come clean with money attitudes that may be destroying the relationship.

The Belief

When a Mistrust Game dynamic begins between people and among families, it becomes a forum for playing out the dark sides of the relationships. For couples, money becomes a channel for maintaining the upper hand in the relationship. Like children at play, a mistrusting partner wants all the blocks in his or her corner. The other partner will often pretend to play along, but then feel justified in hiding his own blocks to maintain some sense of control. Lies become the currency of communication. There is no "our money." There is only "my money."

Based on a latticework of untruths, such relationships generate intense distrust. Partners distrust each other's motives. One thinks the other is out to "get me." When both partners launder money, each treats the other like some enemy or authority figure who must be "gotten around." These partners cheat on their mates with money, but what they are really doing is "doing in the other partner before they themselves get done in."

Sometimes partners in this dynamic, men particularly, believe the conflict might be solved by throwing more money at the situation. They decide to work longer hours or take out bigger loans to solve the problem. But that's like pouring gasoline on the fire, and so the financial tension and mistrust worsens.

Money mistrust is deeply rooted because it has usually lain dormant for many years. Families rarely discuss openly their money doctrines. Barely functional family money systems may have been going on for generations. But until family members have the courage to look at their money beliefs, they are apt to repeat the historical themes time and time again. The end result: As adults, they harbor a strong allegiance to how money was viewed and used in the families they grew up in. Thus, when they move into a relationship, the fight for whose family was right comes into play either consciously or unconsciously if the participants don't approach the subject with a sense of humor and vulnerability.

Parents, grandparents, aunts, and uncles also play this game with their offspring. This version of the game is called the Beyond the Grave Mistrust Game. Shari Lynn's story is a prime example.

Shari Lynn's Story

Shari Lynn was raised on a farm in Arkansas. Her father, Elray, and her mother, Peggy, raised cotton on a small farm near Little Rock. Shari Lynn and her younger brother, Freddie Joe, grew up picking cotton, corn, and watermelon, and their mother took in boarders and raised chickens to help keep food on the table.

When Shari Lynn turned eighteen, she went to beautician school because she loved doing hair. She established a small hair salon in Little Rock, and was taking her time picking a husband from among the local boys, most of whom she said "are just down-home hicks." Freddie Joe, five years her junior, had always loved guns and fighting and couldn't wait to enlist in the Army. He served meritoriously in the 1991 Persian Gulf War, but was later killed as the troops were pulling out.

Shari Lynn's parents were devastated when Freddie Joe died. Her father increased his drinking and died after a few years. Shari Lynn's mother, Peggy, had been a lifelong diabetic from obesity, a trait on her mother's family's side. After Shari Lynn's father died, Peggy became a recluse, eventually developing agoraphobia and being terrified of leaving the house. Within a year, she had eaten herself up to 300 pounds and died when her heart gave out the following year.

Shari Lynn was overwhelmed with the rapid deaths of all of her close family members. About this time, she was contacted by her great-uncle Jeb's lawyer. Uncle Jeb had never married, and he had no heirs for the fortune created by his tire business in Missouri. Great-uncle Jeb hadn't been close to the family, and Shari Lynn's father had always referred to him as "that skinflint, no-good tire salesman."

Suddenly, however, Shari Lynn learned that Great-uncle Jeb was on his deathbed with pneumonia and Alzheimer's disease. He was still lucid enough to will his $20 million fortune to Shari Lynn, his closest living relative. However, whether because of Alzheimer's or just plain "orneriness," he made some unusual stipulations to Shari Lynn's inheritance.

In fact, Shari Lynn was flabbergasted when she read the conditions. First, she was to visit her Great-uncle Jeb in St. Louis each week until he died. Second, she was to become the keeper of the family genealogy and compile the three rooms' worth of family pictures, birth certificates, death certificates, souvenirs, and paraphernalia Great-uncle Jeb had been collecting for fifty years. She was to pull together this information into a family museum to be established in St. Louis alongside his original Jeb's Tire Store Emporium. Third, Shari Lynn was to obtain an undergraduate and master's degree in business from Texas Tech, his alma mater, with special funds set aside in trust.

Finally, Shari Lynn had to get married, bear a son, and name her son Jeb Henry. At the time of the male child's birth, she would inherit the $20 million. There was no time limit on the conditions, but the money would revert in trust to Texas Tech in the event she died without having met the conditions.

At twenty-six, Shari Lynn was overwhelmed by this news. She is still contemplating the offer and whether she has the will and energy to accomplish the demands. At this writing, Uncle Jeb is on life support and near death in St. Louis. $

The Secret

People who fear losing control of their money with their partners and hide it rather than talk about it are fear-based people. They've given in to their fear-based money needs at an extreme level. They live in a paranoid world in which they don't trust anyone with the most important thing to them in the world: money.

Their money almost becomes a spouse or a child to them. A human partner, sibling, or child who tries to come between them and their money will have hell to pay. The Mistrust Game player values money over human relationships. The fearful one controls every aspect of any outsider's connection with "my money," guarding it like a jealous husband or rabid mother.

Parents play this game with their children, too—sometimes even after the parent dies. They control their money even from beyond the grave when they stipulate conditions the heir must fulfill prior to inheritance. Widows and widowers are also controlled from the grave by partners who build in money restrictions regarding remarriage or transference of trusts.

Game Triggers

This game is typically triggered by a paranoid belief in lack and limitation. If and when you make some money, inherit some money, see some potential in getting major amounts of money, and have fear-based money beliefs, this game can be triggered. Some of the common trigger situations are:

- Being taken advantage of or robbed of money as a child
- Being parented with a fearful, "gimme-gimme" approach to managing and handling money
- Watching parents and grandparents war over money
- Being an adult child of estranged parents who stripped each other of wealth during the divorce
- Inheriting sudden money
- Coming face-to-face with your mortality and realizing you "can't take it with you" but you still want to
- Realizing too late you can't change your family money dynamic but you can control the destiny of your money
- Realizing you can control people through your money

Disarming Strategies

Disengaging from the Mistrust Game can take a significant commitment to exploring the source of your fear and paranoia. If you seriously choose to distance yourself from this kind of mistrust, you will need the courage to also see why you distrust yourself so much. Trust begins with yourself. Some of the strategies are:

Trace the origins of your money distrust. Look at pictures of family members in your childhood photo album. Check yourself for any discomfort while viewing the pictures as you quiz yourself about from where or whom you may have acquired your money distrust.

Acknowledge your dependency on money control to feel safe. You will want to explore, with a financial or mental health counselor, where the root of your hypercontrol needs lies. Once explored and processed, you can then start building a trusting relationship first with yourself, then with others around money.

Take a forgiveness moment, for yourself and for anyone else you have chosen to control through money. Affirm the following by filling in the appropriate blanks: "I, (your name), commit to a healthy relationship between my money and myself. I take charge of creating a trusting relationship with my money and with those people in my life that are important to me, including _____. I know that mistrust is learned and that I can learn to trust through right action in my relationships with both my money and others."

Notice when you want to spend money and hide it from someone important in your life. At that time, take a moment and ask yourself, "What is it I am trying to hide? Why do I need to do this at this moment? What is the worst thing that will happen if I come clean with my family member, if I tell the truth about what I want to do *before* I do it?"

Notice when you lie about money when you first form a relationship. Where did it start with your current partner? Your child? Your parent? Another family member?

Your New Way of Thinking

"I will be up front with myself and my loved ones about money. As our relationship improves, this trust will spread throughout all areas of my life."

Your Action Plan

Inner steps to take:

1. Work with your partner as a team to analyze how your family's beliefs, attitudes, and secrets impact your relationship. Think about all of the time and energy you and your partner spend going on money diets, then working harder to earn more, and splurging in hopes of saving your relationship.

2. Identify your money tension and discuss it openly with appropriate family members. Teach them to be responsible for their money behaviors by showing them how it's done. Realize that making more money or controlling your money does not heal or strengthen your relationship.

3. Share the burden for money responsibility in your relationships. Work with a counselor or investment expert to configure your money use or future allocations so everyone has a say in financial expectations and needs.

4. Keep a money mistrust log. Each time you feel compelled to conceal some aspect of money, write down the thought, the emotion behind the thought, and how this would be of service to you or others.

Financial steps to take:

1. Commit to money honesty by setting up your own money trust fund: Put $50 in a jar. For one month, pay yourself $1 each time you tell a money truth. Take away $2 each time you tell a money lie. Keep an accounting of your trust transactions, and then see how rich or poor your money trust is by month's end. Reward or penalize yourself accordingly.

2. Exchange money information with the important people in your life. This includes all data: bank accounts; money investments; insurance policies; tax records; records of house purchase; list of major assets; loan and credit card information; and names of tax preparer, insurance agent, and health insurance advisor.

3. As a couple, organize your financial information. Read Julie Morgenstern's *Organizing from the Inside Out: The Fool-proof System for Organizing Your Home, Your Office, and Your Life*.

4. Set up personal bank accounts for each partner, and one joint account for mutual money. This way, each has control of some of his or her own money, while together they manage the joint money.

5. Hold a fun, once-a-month meeting to talk responsibly with family or partners about money. Make it a joyful occasion and celebrate your talking *through* money issues instead of hiding them. If this proves impossible, set up a meeting with a mediator or a therapist to work with you and your partner toward full disclosure of financial assets, including possible inheritances.

6. Cross-train in household-finance tasks. Every three or six months, switch jobs so that one handles all the money while the other partner is responsible for other domestic duties.

7. Make all meetings with financial advisors into joint sessions. Both partners should go to see the tax advisor, the investment counselor, and the banker.

Think about It

"Prosperity is living easily and happily in the real world, whether you have money or not."

—Jerry Gellis

THE MISTRUST GAME

Rules	Guard my money at all cost. No one can be trusted.
Belief	I can't trust anyone to know my money dealings or be responsible with money, especially family.
Secret	I am afraid my family and friends will abuse me so I have to keep control. No one gets close to me—not even me.
Feeling	Fear, paranoia, mistrust
Game Triggers	Inherited money, having money, finding out you can control with your money
Disarming Strategies	Being honest, coming clean with money lies, establishing open relationships with those you love
Persona	Hoarder
Action	Openness

Chapter Fourteen

Game #12: The Moneyholic Game

Redford and Patty's Story

Redford and Patty, in their early forties, have four children, two boys and two girls. When their first child was born, they purchased land and decided to build their first home. They went into tremendous debt to do this ($400,000), but they wanted their children to be raised in a nice area with all of the positives life has to offer.

Redford was a salesman for a tire company, and Patty was and still is a nurse. Patty worked all during her children's early years so she could give her kids the extra things in life: the best clothes, summer camps each year, and lots of the latest toys. Redford also worked many weekends, so the children often had to stay at one of the grandparents' homes. Within a few years, Redford and Patty had run up about $30,000 in credit-card debt on eight credit cards as a result of furnishing their 5,000-square-foot home, and paying for two cars, an RV, and a summer cabin.

But the couple paid another price as well. Redford typically got home at 7 P.M. or 8 P.M. Usually he headed immediately to the bar for a couple of martinis to kill the day's exhaustion. Patty typically got home late from her ten-hour shifts four days a week. Her mother, Eloise, usually picked up the children from school and fed them dinner, keeping them until Patty and Redford returned from work. Eloise often took over child-care duty when Patty could pick up extra shifts at time and a half.

The four children started learning early about money. They were told, "Mom and Dad work so much because we need to make money to pay our debts and get you kids everything you want." The children learned that money was more important than anything in their family. Little Bobby used to complain when Mom and Dad were away so much. He'd ask, "Mommy and Daddy, can't you stay and see my soccer game today, just this once, please?"

Patty and Redford would explain, "Bobby, we'd love to see you play, but we have to work so you can have soccer clothes and soccer shoes. We'll take you to dinner tomorrow to celebrate, though, to your favorite restaurant. You pick." The family reserved Sundays to eat out at the best restaurants. The tab usually ran to over $150 for the six of them, but Redford always said, "It's worth it since it's family time."

Patty always said she wanted a middle-class life but didn't want her kids to be spoiled. Redford had been an only child and given everything he wanted materially. His father owned a couple of gas stations and was seldom home, but he bought Redford the newest pinball machines, go-karts, and motorcycles. Redford's father also taught him to play cards. This was one of the rare occasions he spent time with his father.

Redford knew his father made an annual trip to Las Vegas to play cards. He recalls his father usually came back with a bundle. Redford always got lots of presents or a new bike or motorbike when his father made "big wins." Redford was usually sent away to an expensive summer camp. He usually left right after school ended in June, then returned a day before school began in September. Sadly, Redford's father passed away after a visit to a casino in Reno one summer when Redford was eighteen. His father was only fifty, but he had a bad heart from "money stress," Redford's father had always said.

As with his own father, Redford rewarded his children and

himself with money. Patty resisted this but was ultimately not averse to running up huge credit-card debts to pay for the six-person family to live well. At least once a year, Patty would drag Redford away from work and load the whole family into the RV for a family trip or at least a few days at the cabin. These jaunts usually lasted no more than five days or so because neither parent could spare the time. The children enjoyed these trips for the most part because they got to spend time with their mom and dad.

One Friday, the unthinkable happened. Redford was laid off when his tire firm merged with a Big 3 tire company. He was out of work for the first time in his forty years, and he was completely shocked. The second-best salesman in his region, he was down-sized to make way for a national sales staff from the larger company.

Redford and Patty grew depressed. They were now $35,000 in debt on their credit cards, and had a home loan of $290,000 after years of paying on it. Redford's health coverage and insurance policies were cancelled. Patty increased her shifts, working six days a week. Redford papered the area with resumes, but after three months had still not found work. The situation was beginning to look pretty bad. Redford stopped looking for work after a while, basically sleeping until 10 or 11 A.M. He stopped shaving and generally moped around the house. He refused to see a doctor and slid into a major depression.

Redford's only pleasure was his Friday-night poker games with his other laid-off buddies. Soon, Redford and a buddy had the idea to blow off the amateur game and head out to the local Indian reservation for a night of real gambling. Redford made about $100 that night and came home to take Patty and the children out for dinner.

Redford felt better for the first time in months. He felt energized and alive. He got a surge out of beating the other players and loved the excitement in the casino. It seemed a long way off from his debts and depression at home. "I may be able to make some money at this," he mused. "I'm a good player. I can make this work and I can get us out of debt, too."

He began using some of Patty's money that he found in the grocery fund in the kitchen. About noon, he'd head out to the casino. Often he lost everything, but a few times he hit very big and came home with a load of bills. For a few months, he got home before Patty's work shift ended, and she never knew what was going on, although she wondered how the grocery money disappeared so fast. Redford always told her he was using the money to take people to lunch, looking for work. Soon the grocery money wasn't enough. He cashed in his unemployment checks for a time, then began borrowing money from his mother and buddies.

Soon, Redford established credit in his favorite casino. Within a few more months, he'd run up about $50,000 in gambling debts. When he couldn't pay, the casino came after Redford and Patty's house and cars. That's when Patty found out the extent of Redford's addiction to gambling. Nearing a breakdown, Patty took the kids and moved home to her parents. She then filed for a legal separation.

Redford was devastated. He begged her to return and said, "I'll do anything to change and get my family back again." Patty's parents took pity on the couple and paid for some marital and debt counseling to help the family come to terms with their money problems.

Ultimately, Patty and Redford sold their house, filed for bankruptcy, reunited as a family, and moved to a duplex owned by Patty's parents. Redford found work at an auto parts store and Patty continued at the hospital. Currently Redford continues in long-term treatment for depression and a gambling addiction. He attends a gambling addiction group every two days and has begun to sponsor other addicts on their road to recovery. Patty gave up using credit cards and is working well with cash.

Today, Redford says with moist eyes, "I was addicted to money and gambling, and I know it. It's a disease for me and I'll have to fight it every day of my life from now on. Patty and I realized we made money our number-one priority in life. But we realized it wasn't making us happy. Now, I have three years of sobriety from my addictions, and life feels good, even though I don't have much to show for it financially. But I have my kids and my beautiful wife. They are the most important things to me."

After five years of rehabilitation, the couple is finally stabilizing. They gave up everything financially, but they say they also learned some very difficult lessons in money addiction. They are also doing their best not to pass on their problems to their children. $

The Moneyholic Game: Buy, Buy, Buy

The Moneyholic Game is a nationwide addiction that mesmerizes most of us to some degree. Children born since 1950 have very little experience with lack and limitation. We have lived with multiplying abundance. Money-generating acumen is not only a source of pride in our social and commerce systems, but it is one of the highest values we hold today. Unfortunately, we have also been seduced by money at many levels through this value system.

We acquire goods to keep us in good social standing. We worship regularly at the altar of the local ATM machine. We give regularly to the unworthy cause of credit-card company profit, and while we used to tithe to charities or churches, now our tithes go out in the form of interest payments. We allow corporate advertisements to coerce us into living a life of desire. These marketing gurus know precisely which strings to pull within us to provoke the greatest response.

If it's not the advertising media exhorting us to spend, it's family members and friends preaching the benefits of buying. They warn us that if we don't buy now we will forfeit precious memories and experiences. "Your kids are young only once," they remind us, or "You'll be too old to enjoy taking that trip to Europe later." Soon we're faced with emotional pressure to prove we're a good spouse or parent. How? By buying something expensive for that special someone. If we don't follow the herd mentality in spending, we are branded "losers" and may very well be made fun of.

Our economy is now heavily dependent on consumers buying goods and services. As Natalie Jenkins and her colleagues point out in *You Paid How Much for That?*, "More than 70% of our gross domestic product is based on what consumers purchase. Our jobs depend on people using credit to buy, buy, and buy more." Therefore we are encouraged and even entreated to play the Moneyholic Game.

We buy. And if we can't afford cash, we charge it—again and again. We never get enough because modern commerce runs on the premise that we can never get enough. Our commercial culture isn't based merely on satisfying our desires through shopping. Instead, it is based on the creation of yet more desires: The more we want, the more we want to want.

So we are caught up in a web of wishes, temporary fulfillment, and longing. Our desire becomes insatiable. Our addiction to money and the things we think it gets us becomes a voracious monster. The Moneyholic Game is alive and well and most of us are addicted.

The Belief

The Moneyholic Game is based on continuous buying behavior, often on credit, or obsessive attempts to obtain money through deal making or other money-based activities like gambling. The thrill is from snagging a win or a windfall. Debt-ridden shoppers, gamblers, and kleptomaniacs all share the fact that they get "high" when they "complete" their transactions. They live for the "money moment"— when the money changes hands, when they break the bank, or when they step outside the store with a new shirt or blouse stuffed inside their coat.

With the advent of day trading, many people have transferred their greedy tendencies to the stock market. In a supposedly legitimate manner, we try to conceal our out-of-control desires with the illusion of investing in stocks. Even if we are only holding on to these new stock purchases for a few moments, we rationalize the legitimacy of our actions by saying that "investing is not an addiction." We are locked into believing more will fill us up inside and make us feel whole and loved.

This belief is based on the premise that money is everything. It will make us feel good, make us feel important, and get us everything we want. We are addicted to the power we think money holds for us. And we have to get, spend, or win money to get back that power each time.

The moneyholic belief system is rooted in using money as others use alcohol, cocaine, or sex. It's a channel for pleasure and pain, because, of course, the underlying dynamic is that the Moneyholic Game is dual in nature. It has a masochistic element to it because the pleasure it offers is momentary while the pain often goes on and on. Moneyholics get accustomed to both the pleasure and the pain—and they are both habit forming.

The Secret

The not-so-secret secret of the Moneyholic Game is that practically our entire society has the disease. It's the addiction of our era. Most of us were raised to play the Moneyholic Game, and antidotes are in short supply because almost everyone else is an addict, too. It's a society-endorsed addiction with a very dark quality to it.

Lots of this money addiction shows up in prison. Some estimates are that as many of 80 percent of all prisoners are there because of money-related crimes. Other than an outdated welfare system, we provide very little support or recovery for moneyholics who go too far with the game.

Another facet to this game is the alarming rise of consumer debt. The average American has a credit-card debt of more than $8,000. At the current interest rates, if that typical cardholder makes the minimum payment each month, the debt won't get paid off for almost fifty years. Americans now have nearly $700 billion in credit-card debt rolling over from month to month. These numbers are staggering.

The vicious secret of the Moneyholic Game is that once we are hooked, unless we become independently wealthy or radically change our money behavior, we probably are hooked for life. With the amount of debt we have, consumerism has ensnared us until death—or bankruptcy—do us part.

Game Triggers

The Moneyholic Game has triggers almost everywhere we look. Almost every engine, piece of equipment, appliance, technology component, automobile, and article of clothing is built to fall apart, rust, break down, or become obsolete within just a few years—or in some cases, months. Our economy is based on obsolescence, and we have to spend more just to keep up.

The Moneyholic Game is also triggered by almost every life stage at our and our family's development. These include, but are not limited to:

- Buying our next car, house, refrigerator, or other big-ticket item. In our society, each of these purchases used to happen every decade or so, but now seem to have been accelerated to every few years.
- Moving through a life change: entering college, graduating from college, getting married or divorced, having children or launching children to college or adulthood, downsizing for retirement
- Getting a raise—this typically triggers a *buy, buy, buy* reaction rather than a *save, save, save* reaction in most of us.
- Getting a temporary win or winning streak
- Suddenly seeing neighbors, close friends, or relatives obtaining something we want (SUV, European vacation, new piece of jewelry, new stock portfolio)
- Feeling less than American because we don't play the Moneyholic Game, thus causing those around us to squirm and feel uncomfortable

Disarming Strategies

Disarming strategies can be complicated. Unfortunately, when basic money-management skill building is required, our money ignorance comes front and center. Some of the basic strategies for confronting moneyholism usually include the following:

First, get real with yourself regarding your assets and liabilities. If you add your total assets (property, cars, stocks, bonds, savings accounts, retirement funds, and income) and subtract your total liabilities (outstanding loans and debts), you will get a clear picture of where you stand. If your liabilities are more than 80 percent of your assets, you are likely a moneyholic.

Next, account for all your credit card debt. Add up everything you own on credit. If it is more than three months' income, you may be headed toward or already be in the Moneyholic Game.

You should also look closely at your debt-payoff schedule. If you will need more than two years to pay off all credit-card and revolving debt, you must take action to use your money more intelligently and get out from under killing debt.

Notice how many times a month you participate in money deals, gambling, or money addiction behaviors. If you have more than one in a month, be sure to take the Moneyholic Assessment at the end of the chapter to assess your level of impulsivity.

If you are a shopaholic, make a list of everything purchased over a three-month period. List these items in three columns: "Critically Needed," "Needed but Could Have Deferred," and "Wanted but Didn't Need." Note in which columns most items fall. Then ask, "What is my payoff for giving myself these things? What do I think would have happened if I hadn't?"

One sign of a moneyholic problem: If you find yourself adjusting your assets toward more risk to try to make up for your debts, you are in danger. Stop this way of thinking and work with a financial advisor to reassess your risk. If you continually feel pressured by peers into doing something with your money that makes you feel uncomfortable so they will feel better, take that as a warning sign as well.

Your New Way of Thinking

"I will not follow the lemmings blindly off the money cliff. I choose instead to be responsible with my money. I will follow my heart and soul, knowing that I am valuable regardless of how much money I have. From now on I will be true to myself."

Your Action Plan

Inner steps to take:

1. Identify the feeling that accompanies your action as a moneyholic—such as happy, sad, or angry. Now view yourself as a ten-year-old child sitting before you. Ask the child: What is wrong and why are you behaving this way? Reassure yourself that you are now an adult and no longer need to make money to try to comfort this ten-year-old. If you are inclined, seek out a therapist for more insight into these moneyholic behaviors.

2. Take the Moneyholic Assessment at the end of the chapter to determine your level of money use. Then come up with a one-year and five-year plan for getting control of your money habits.

3. Put yourself on a short leash credit-wise by resolving to use credit only as a last resort. Think your purchases through first. Many expensive purchases are made impulsively. Also, don't borrow to pay off other debts. Trying to do so usually fails, and you may end up increasing your debt.

Financial steps to take:

1. Track your spending for at least three months. Know where your money is going so you can tell if you're spending more than you need on clothing, entertainment, gifts, and other luxury items. Once you're aware of your negative spending habits, you can revise them accordingly. One good way to do that is to study your expenses on a weekly basis and resolve to cut one more nonessential purchase each week.

2. Start reducing your debt. This requires setting definable goals. For instance, decide how much debt you would like to pay off within a certain time. Then you can establish rules that will help you achieve those goals.

3. Try this two-step approach to getting out of debt: (1) Every month pay *double* the minimum monthly payment on your credit card; (2) Don't charge another penny. If you can manage these two steps, your card likely will be paid off in a few years, instead of thirty years!

4. Or, use this debt strategy: Ask your employer to deposit your paycheck directly into your checking account. Then instruct your bank to make an automatic monthly payment to the card issuer on a specific date every month that is double the minimum payment on your current bill. Most banks will make this arrangement, and it's easiest if you're paying your bills online. Then put away your credit card and don't use it except in emergencies.

5. If you think you've acquired discipline, take out a home-equity loan instead of credit cards. The interest paid on a loan up to $100,000 is deductible as long as you itemize your deductions. *Caution:* If you don't pay back this loan, you could put your home in jeopardy.

6. Identify what provides the thrill for you in money matters. Then set about doing just the opposite. Choose boring over exciting. Invest, say, in mutual funds rather than individual stocks; shun margin buying and instead make cash-only

equity purchases. Buy a used car for cash rather than a new one on credit. Vacation at an affordable domestic resort rather than a chic but expensive foreign one.

Think about It

"If you make money your god, it will plague you like the devil."

—Henry Fielding

THE MONEYHOLIC GAME	
Rules	Buy, buy, buy no matter what. Win, win, win money no matter what.
Belief	Having, getting, or winning—no matter the cost—will make me happy.
Secret	I am drowning, and my debt owns me.
Feeling	Continuously empty; money, please feed me.
Game Triggers	Life changes, entering the consumer society, valuing money above everything else
Disarming Strategies	Get a clear picture of your total financial picture and debt, as well as any addictive, self-destructive behaviors.
Persona	Addict
Action	Take control of your money habits and get into recovery for money addiction.

Moneyholic Assessment

After the following statements, write *T* for those that are true for you, and *F* for those that are false.

1. Watching my money grow or adding up my investments makes me feel good. ____
2. I go on shopping binges periodically. ____
3. I love the initial high that comes with spending money or being with others when they spend theirs. ____
4. I regularly like to gamble because it is so exciting. ____
5. I find that I can't go a day without spending money somehow, somewhere. ____

6. I simply can't budget. It's too restrictive. ____
7. I have at least one credit card that has reached its maximum balance and I can't pay it off. ____
8. I don't have enough money for emergencies. I just keep my fingers crossed. ____
9. I bounce checks or pay my bill late sometimes. ____
10. I don't really know where my money goes. ____
11. If I want something, I buy it whether I can afford it or not. ____
12. I would put a vacation on my credit card knowing I couldn't pay it off. ____
13. I often feel guilty about how much I spend. ____
14. I have to have others bail me out financially sometimes. ____
15. I scramble to get my taxes paid each year and am usually surprised at how much I have to pay. ____

If you answered more than six of these as true, you may be playing a Moneyholic Game.

Chapter Fifteen

Game #13: The Slave Game

Jeff and Joe's Story

Jeff and Joe took very different paths. Jeff worked in lower management at a large technology company. He had worked himself up to management after being an assembly-line employee for ten years; he was now thirty-five and managed many of the people he formerly worked with on the line. Jeff's real passion, however, was deep-sea fishing. He longed to own his own boat and take anglers out on a daily basis. Jeff already took his kids fishing on overnight runs at least once a month.

Joe had worked with Jeff on the assembly line and also had been promoted to a lower-middle management position at this same firm. Joe was single and in his early thirties; he had no short-term plans for a wife or children. Joe enjoyed writing and had taken occasional night courses at the community adult school and junior college to perfect his skills. His passion was writing novels about his experiences growing up with his grandparents in the South African outback country.

Unlike Jeff, Joe had been saving for the day when he would quit his job with two years' expenses in the bank and forge ahead in his new profession as a writer. Joe saw his current job as a means to an end but nothing more. Joe told Jeff he would eventually go crazy if he had to deal much longer with the pressure of being caught between upper management and the assembly employees. He was adamant that he would cut the umbilical chord and start his new career. He always complained that he didn't have the energy after working twelve-hour days, six days a week, to follow his writing passion, but now his writing professors said he was maturing as an artist. With almost two years' expenses in the bank, Joe felt it was time to try his wings.

After Joe left the company, he and Jeff would get together every month to catch up. Jeff was shocked at the tiny apartment Joe had moved into in order to live his dream. Joe explained, "There are no more fancy weekend trips or fine dining. I'm committed to finishing my first novel."

Jeff envied Joe's enthusiasm for his new career, especially when Joe made statements like, "I've never been more alive or happy in my life." On the other hand, Jeff told Joe that, "I feel like it's a combat zone at work. Upper management is demanding I fire a bunch of employees to keep the company afloat. The first shift crew is always complaining about the lack of support from the company. I've even got a new ulcer." Jeff bemoaned that he had no choice but to stay, with his mortgage and family expenses: "I'm stuck. My dream of owning a fishing boat is a long way off, Joe."

Five years later, Jeff had moved to middle management at the same company. He still nursed his fishing dream, but he was now forty and his kids were heading off to college. Joe had been writing for several years but had returned to work part time at the old company as a relief supervisor. He was still trying to get that first novel published. Jeff was glad to see his old friend back at work, even for only a few days a week. Joe, however, thought to himself, "Gee, Jeff has aged a good ten years. He's gray and everything."

When Jeff asked Joe if he wished he had kept his old position, Joe said, "No, I'm still happier today pursuing my passion making less money than I would have been making four or five times as much." Jeff grimaced, and asked himself, "I wonder how things would have been if I had quit, too. Would I have had two or more rigs by this time?"

Two years later, their employer terminated both men's jobs as part of a downsizing. Joe was secretly glad, but Jeff was incensed and went through a year of lawsuits. With his settlement, he finally bought a half interest in a small fishing boat. He takes the rig out most days, but he has to limit his time on the sea due to hypertension and bypass surgery. His doctor says the years with the company cost him his health.

Joe returned to writing and finally sold that novel. Joe was happy that he hadn't wasted seven years plugging away full time. He looks about ten years younger than Jeff. Joe sometimes sails with his friend Jeff, recalling the "old days of technology." $

The Slave Game: Trapped by Your Job

The Slave Game taps into our deep-seated safety and physiological needs. Those who play this game enslave themselves to the job, believing the money safety it offers will keep the wolves from the door. They typically overwork and sacrifice their personal goals and happiness for their jobs and families.

They often feel trapped. They may have outgrown their dead-end jobs, but circumstances and their terror of risk taking keep them bound in what feels safe. Slave Game players sometimes have a martyr streak. It comfortably keeps them in a one-down position. A martyrdom dynamic also ensures that their family and friends know how miserable they are. Many times their financial commitments and responsibilities make them believe they have no choices. They think they must grin and bear it. They suffer through life and an unsatisfying job. They also hear plenty of stories of friends who have risked and failed, who followed their hearts only to go bankrupt a year later.

The Belief

Slave Game players root their future in their jobs and organizations. They believe the self-sacrifice makes them good providers, honorable spouses, long-suffering parents, and loyal sons and daughters. But the price can be very high. They labor under the belief that pain is the way to gain. They defer their own pleasure, usually for a lifetime. Often their dreams die inside them.

They often swallow a seething anger when they become lifetime slaves. They internalize their passion, and this can turn to resentment, anger, and, later, illness. Cancer, heart disease, diabetes, and strokes can all result from a lifetime of unrelenting responsibility. They may subvert their dreams to the degree they become depressed or worse, even end their own lives because the future appears bleak. The Slave Game literally sucks the life out of them. Instead of their income offering long-term nurturing, it saps their energy, their strength, their essence.

The Secret

The belief that if we have a solid job and money safety, life will be all right, is a little like the film *The Money Pit*. In that movie, no matter how much money Tom Hanks and Shelley Long sink into their beloved old house, it ends up costing them more. They buy the house thinking it will bring them ultimate happiness. They stretch themselves financially and work night and day to keep up with the horrific repairs. Every fix turns up a dozen new problems, however. The house becomes the Home from Hell. Tom nearly suffers a nervous breakdown.

Therein lies the nasty secret of the Slave Game. We've given up ownership. Instead, we are owned—by our houses, our cars, our credit cards, our furniture, our children's educations, and more. We're on a short leash; our jobs have become our masters.

Material goods and what we think is a solid job alone will not deliver the eternal satisfaction we are chasing. In the Slave Game, we sacrifice our inner longings in order to be responsible, grown-up, and well intentioned. We believe that we have to choose between being passionate and being adult. We thought we had to martyr the passion to become the realist. We've become gravely responsible. In fact, our fear of failing and avoidance of the dream makes us old, exhausted, and depleted.

But we misunderstand. We believe it's a choice between two evils. In fact, life is meant to be a happy merger of two possibilities for joy—passion and responsibility. When we become balanced, passionate adults, we enact our joy in responsible ways. We make our lives a living heaven, instead of a working hell.

Game Triggers

The Slave Game is one many of us play because we've been raised to believe it is often the measure of our commitment. It's triggered whenever that parental persona inside us (the superego that recites the things your mother and dad always lectured you about) rears its ugly head, when you:

- Leave home and feel you have to start "living like an adult"
- Get your first bank account, credit card, or bill
- Start your first job
- Start your first small business, even a lemonade stand at age eleven
- Go on your first date and are embarrassed you can't drive yet or don't own a car
- Become engaged, get married, have your first child, or Mom and Dad refuse to give you any more handouts
- Get your first wave of grownup guilt—e.g., when you realize you don't have enough for a down payment for that Volkswagen, when you want to buy your date a present but can't afford it, or when you have your first child and can't buy your own home yet

Disarming Strategies

Disarming from the Slave Game takes a soul-searching look at what you want and don't want in your life. Start by making a list of your life dreams and goals in the short term (one year) and longer term (three to five years).

Next, assess how satisfied you are in your current job on a scale of 1 to 10, with 1 being *very unsatisfied* and 10 being *very satisfied*. Once you know your satisfaction level, make two columns on a piece of paper: "What Gives Me Satisfaction in My Current Job" and "What Makes Me Dissatisfied in My Current Job." Fill in as many items under each column as you can think of.

Now that you have an idea of how much (or how little) your job is fulfilling your dreams and making you satisfied, proceed to the Action Plan below.

Your New Way of Thinking

"There is no such thing as safety, so why shouldn't I pursue my passion? How I spend my time and money is a reflection of me. Only by identifying the reality of who I am can I achieve joyous, responsible action with money."

Your Action Plan

Inner steps to take:

1. Write your obituary, but write it this way: "Here lies (your name). By being a slave to responsibility, he/she deprived the world of . . ."

2. Beware of turning into a martyr and sacrificing your deepest desires. Determine how you can comfortably coexist with your job and money, then try to do it.

3. Ask yourself, "What benefit do I get from worrying about my work and my money? What bad things might happen if

I stopped worrying?" Give yourself from fifteen minutes to a half hour to worry about your security and money in a clear, focused way. Do nothing else. Then do the same the next day at the same time. Do this for one week to see if focused worrying freed you up for more joy in your life. The following week, limit your worry to ten minutes, then decrease the worry period until it's gone.

4. Be realistic. Honor your financial responsibilities, but seek to find a way to also pursue your deepest goals. This means you may have to go to school at night to pursue your interests, or work two jobs until you can feasibly make the transition. Discuss with your spouse or partner a plan whereby he or she works while you study. Then switch, with you taking over household duties while your partner pursues a passion they've had for years.

5. Identify your essential material needs, but then allow yourself some frivolous money to spend as you like, as long as you stay within your budget. Balance your responsibility with joy. Find some ways to take pleasure in your own accomplishments, creations, or dreams.

6. Work at shifting your need for approval from outside to inside yourself. Listen to your own yearnings, then choose a prudent course to make them a reality. Follow true passions after you have wisely surveyed the situation at hand.

Financial steps to take:

1. Make a massive cutback in your lifestyle in order to build a reserve. Once you have a six-month reserve, take on a second job that you enjoy. When you have two years' reserve, quit the first job entirely. Do whatever is necessary to make this arrangement work, whether it's moving out of your apartment into a furnished room or eating macaroni and cheese instead of steak.

2. Develop a personal mission statement. Each day at work, ask yourself if you are furthering your mission, if you are doing what you believe you were created to do.

Think about It

"Man must choose whether to be rich in things or in the freedom to use them."

—Ivan Illich, *Deschooling Society*

THE SLAVE GAME	
Rules	Enslave myself to a job or profession in order to feel OK about myself and my commitments.
Belief	I have to sacrifice myself in order to be responsible. My passions are frivolous.
Secret	I hate doing this work and am angry at all the people that are dependent on me. I feel punished, but it hurts so good.
Feeling	Used, punished
Game Triggers	Being made to feel responsible, inadequate, or martyred
Disarming Strategies	Own your resentment and anger. Take charge of combining your sense of commitment with your passion in a balanced way.
Persona	Martyr
Action	Take stock of how much of yourself you are giving away. Balance the pain and pleasure in your life, and shoot for more pleasure and joyfulness in fulfilling your creative as well as your responsible nature.

Part III

Playing a New Way

Chapter Sixteen

Game #14: The Giving Game

Tucker and Beverly's Story

When they were kids, Tucker and his two brothers pursued scientific projects. As the three grew up, they continued their creative hobbies, and as young adults, they built and sold some of the first whirlpool bathtubs mass-produced in the United States. The brothers wanted to build something to help people relax after a long day at work, and they succeeded by inventing one of our most valued modern conveniences.

In the late 1980s, the brothers sold their firm to a large recreation and leisure company. They each made millions of dollars. While the other brothers went on to make new investments, Tucker was the only one to get out of the business and retire at a young age with his $20 million share. Tucker remained a humble, giving man. He still loved to tinker with things, and he continued to date the same down-to-earth woman, Beverly, whom he'd been with before the sale of the company.

About the only thing that changed about Tucker was that he bought a new twin-engine plane that could get him to where he wanted to go a little faster. Tucker could have afforded a Lear jet, but he felt it was too extravagant despite his wealth. Instead he bought a mid-level, personal plane and loved to fly it. A few years later, Tucker married Beverly, and they continued to live in their modest home where they had lived before he acquired this huge sum of money.

After he married Beverly, Tucker increased his giving. Instead of giving away several hundred dollars a month to a charity or someone in need, the couple began giving away $25,000 a month. Beverly liked to read the newspaper and would search the local area for people or charities in need. Then she and Tucker would send them a cashier's check. Beverly and Tucker also liked giving anonymous gifts to those who hadn't solicited them or who were just down on their luck and in need of assistance. The couple also had a strongly balanced spiritual life to go along with their material side. They had regular spiritual practices, and part of their daily practice was to give thanks for their incredible abundance.

Interestingly, they began to observe an odd thing happening. The more money Tucker and Beverly gave away, the more they seemed to get back. They never hoarded but simply put the money back into circulation. With Tucker and Beverly, money just seemed to flow, bringing health and wealth to many others in the world. Over the next ten years, Tucker created two more companies. These were also purchased by large corporations, and Tucker and Beverly's net worth doubled again.

However, they remained content with a modest lifestyle. They didn't participate in negative Money Games particularly, although Tucker was aware that he might slip occasionally into the mind-set of a wealthy person. He said he would catch himself, hopefully before he offended anyone.

With their additional wealth, however, Tucker and Beverly did change one thing: They created the Tuck Foundation and upped their monthly giving to $100,000. The foundation became famous for contributing and installing whirlpool devices in senior citizen centers around the world. When asked about the extent of his giving, Tucker said, "It's simply the right thing to do. We've been blessed, and I think it's part of our contribution in life to bless others as best we can." $

The Giving Game: Making a Difference

The Giving Game is based on an outflow and inflow dynamic. It involves channeling our resources in a positive flow of energy back out into the world. The resources vary, including skills we have to offer in volunteer work; contributions we make in time, energy, or sponsorship; and the outflow of money, goods, and a multitude of other items. The contributions can be small, maybe just a few hours a year, say, serving Thanksgiving dinner to the homeless, or contributing $5 to the local Boys and Girls Club. Or the contribution could be something as grand as endowing millions in cash or property. The point is, no matter to what extent, those who play the Giving Game believe in the value of giving as a way to continue the flow. When we participate in the Giving Game in a positive way, we extend our belief that our resources and talents make a difference outside ourselves.

In fact, though, we also make a difference *inside* ourselves when we give. The Giving Game involves a quid pro quo similar to what we've explored in other Money Games. That is, money is a channel of energy. In and of itself, it has no owner. It simply resides with us individually for a time, then flows somewhere else. It comes into our pockets, then goes out again; and it returns to us yet again according to our belief system and money practices. We give, we get. We get, we give back, if we choose to continue the circulation.

To create a positive flow, giving needs to be first worked out in the home where we live. This is our first way to express a balance between the proper inflow and outflow of money. Here, we can first experiment with participating in the right ways of giving by using money lovingly with family members. Our motives and intentions are clear, based on unselfish acts of kindness. We check our motives before giving to make sure there are no ulterior motives such as manipulating people into doing what we want with the promise of money as a reward. In our families we learn to share. We choose to forgive and let go of past mistakes we have made with money and give from a pure heart based on goodwill, which nourishes our soul.

When the soul is nourished, we are then able to cooperate as one, and giving results naturally. Through giving we dissolve our separateness. When we share we become one with all of humanity. Our hearts and minds open up, and goodwill is restored. We teach and live based on adequate and charitable giving. Through modeling for our children and others, we master the concept of sharing and take this vision globally as we attempt to heal the people in the world who suffer from famine and hardship.

The Belief

One of the interesting things about the Giving Game is that on the surface we may appear altruistic and self-sacrificing. But the reality is that we still are getting our needs met through this act of giving. Not only do we feel better about ourselves when we give, we reap some personal benefit from the act of giving. The clarity with which we understand our intent in giving will therefore determine the authenticity of our giving.

In other words, our personal belief system about giving still underlies our "selfless" acts. Despite our best intent, there is still a component of selfish motivation to giving. This is human nature. When we understand the selfish part of selflessness, we get closer to authentic giving, with fewer and fewer strings attached.

If we look at the hierarchy of needs discussed earlier, the Giving Game often gets played out as the following:

Physiological and survival needs (food, water, shelter, warmth). When our needs are focused here, we may find ourselves giving at a very basic level. For example, a family of four may only have $300 a month to spend on food, but their contribution of $10 in canned goods to the local homeless shelter each month can be a difficult, but rewarding, sacrifice, a demonstration of the family's commitment to service. The family feels better giving because perhaps there is an acknowledgement that there are others who are worse off, and the donors can be of service, no matter how small the gift.

Safety needs (security, stability, freedom from fear). These needs can show up in how our giving gets motivated by fear, such as an outpouring of blankets and food after a flood or fire situation, or giving cash to provide for orphans following a devastating earthquake. The destructiveness can trigger our own safety fears. We project our selflessness outward while feeling safer ourselves because we take action to overcome the fear for both ourselves and others.

Belonging and social needs (friends, family, spouse, lover relationships). These needs can manifest in giving acts if the gifts allow us the opportunity to serve in groups or social situations. We like giving but we also enjoy the social aspect of being involved in giveback situations. We may more often volunteer or give as part of a group, rather than anonymously or individually, because we benefit socially from the unity of giving.

Esteem and ego status needs (achievement, mastery, recognition, respect). These needs are met in giving in which our contributions and endowments are recognized. That is, we get identified as the donor and reap recognition because of it.

Self-actualization needs (pursuit of inner talent, creativity, fulfillment). These needs express themselves through contributions that we feel compelled to make as part of our commitment to service. These include anonymous endowments; volunteering for a great length of time; an arduous commitment, such as a nurse using her two-week vacation to treat sick children in Somalia; or just a long-term commitment to service at a local hospice or senior center over several years. Again the selflessness of the acts still creates an inflow of positive results for us as we self-actualize.

So the belief system behind the Giving Game is that giving ful-
fills a need for ourselves as well as others. As givers, we give first,
but typically we give knowing that in doing so, we also get back
something for ourselves. The reality of this dynamic is that very few
of us would give without some payoff for ourselves. This is not to
say that giving is negative. But the intent behind our giving says a
lot about our belief structure, and if we are caught up in an
extremely self-oriented giving dynamic, our positive intent can get
skewed. Our giving acts can then get muddled up in a web of
giving secrets.

The Secret

As is true of the other Money Games explored in this book, the
Giving Game has both positive and negative aspects to it. The oft-
told, anonymous "Story of the Spoons" can illustrate:

> There once was a holy man who died and was met by St.
> Peter at heaven's gate. Peter said to the man, "My son, you
> have lived a dedicated life, helping the poor and the wealthy
> alike. You have the opportunity now to see both purgatory and
> heaven before you go to your eternal place."
>
> In the blink of an eye, Peter and the holy man found them-
> selves in purgatory. They stood in a great banquet hall where a
> splendid table was laid with every type of food and drink.
> Around the table sat a large group of people, each holding a
> golden spoon in their hands with a long golden handle that
> stretched out more than two feet from their arms. Sadly, the
> people were weeping and crying from hunger. No matter how
> much food they scooped up in their golden spoons, the han-
> dles were too long to allow any food to reach their lips.
>
> In another blink, Peter and the holy man found them-
> selves in heaven in a great banquet hall almost identical to the
> one in purgatory. Again, a great feast was laid, and around the
> table sat a group of people holding large golden spoons with

two-foot handles. But instead of weeping, the banqueters were laughing and singing. As the holy man watched them, they were scooping up the beautiful food and feeding it to their neighbors across the table. All were joyfully fed.

The "Story of the Spoons" illustrates two important points: One, that giving involves a cycle of receiving and sending. Two, that there is always some payoff for giving. In heaven, people were feeding others in order that they themselves might be fed. To deny the taking part of this giving dynamic is to be blind to the reality of the duality that we live in, particularly with money.

We have a dual nature. That is, we experience an inner world and an outer world. In life, we try to manage those two aspects of ourselves so that we can find fulfillment and happiness. Neither is all good or all bad. Both holy men and unholy men have to live, feed, sleep, and be clothed. To deny that saints have human needs like clothing or shelter is to deny the reality of human life. To deny that the regular guy on the street doesn't need an inner life of sustenance is to deny the reality of personal evolution. Giving helps us more clearly see the merger of the inner and outer duality.

The key is to give out of honest intent. It is to know why, how, when, and where we give as part of our own evolution. The negative aspect of the Giving Game bubbles up when our selfish intent belies the obvious good we do by giving. On the hierarchy of needs, these negative aspects can look like this:

Physiological and survival needs (food, water, shelter, warmth). If we give from a fear for our self-survival, our secret intent may be to keep the wolves from our own door by projecting the fear elsewhere. If we donate or give from a place of fear or guilt, we create a dynamic of lack. If we give from a place of trust and without thought for our own safety and survival, then we are trusting in the energy to come back to us.

Safety needs (security, stability, freedom from fear). When we give to panhandlers on the street, for example, because their presence is unnerving and we want them simply to go away, we operate out of an intent for safety and security, not from altruism. When we can give to the homeless by making contact with them through more than just money, perhaps volunteering to work with them, feed them, or simply provide them with conversation, we see them as people, not as a menace to our own security and freedom.

Belonging and social needs (friends, family, spouse, lover relationships). When we contribute or volunteer because our names are on the wall along with other volunteers, or our social group becomes the volunteer network, we may operate from disguised intent. The socializing takes priority over the volunteer work.

Esteem and ego status needs (achievement, mastery, recognition, respect). When we make contributions and endowments to leave a monument to ourselves, have our name in the society pages, or assuage a hidden guilt about having so much money, we again may be unconscious about our mixed purposes. Or we simply are very obvious in using giving as a screen for getting more business and status.

Self-actualization needs (pursuit of inner talent, creativity, fulfillment). We may give as part of our own self-actualization and evolution as enlightened beings. But if we need to show that we're "rising above the fray with our good deeds," we may be living out of a "holiness persona" that serves us on an ego-gratification level but not on an actualization level.

The essence of playing a positive Giving Game is to play it without secrets. It is to play with clear intent, with few strings attached. It is not to give just to earn approval, respect, or deference. The truly positive giver cares not if there are witnesses to his or her largesse. Truly positive givers value their individuality enough to be true to themselves.

Game Triggers

The Giving Game can be triggered for a variety of positive and negative reasons.

- Altruism
- Guilt
- Newfound wealth
- Fear of the future, fear of eternity, fear of God
- Economic reward for giving (tax or corporate benefits)
- Religion
- Morals
- Collective concern
- Manipulation by others (influenced donations)
- Desire for social contact
- Boredom
- Avocation
- Avoidance of home life
- Social responsibility

Many of these triggers come into play with both the positive and negative sides of our needs on the hierarchy. The secret to responding appropriately to the triggers is to base our actions on authentic, centered giving whenever possible.

Disarming Strategies

To play the Giving Game straight, we need to look at our deepest motivations. This means asking the WIIFM question with each gift: "What's in it for me and is that the primary reason I'm giving?" It means choosing the best action and getting real with ourselves about whether the true benefit of giving is to ourselves or to others.

We must ask ourselves if our giving is motivated by other desires. For example, are we motivated mostly to lower our income taxes? Are we driven to relieve our guilt caused by acts of selfishness, such as paying our employees less than they deserve? Are we interested purely in gaining favorable recognition from society based on our giving?

We must analyze the intent behind the gift and how and what type of gift we are sharing. One way to explore this is to experience the poor, the homeless, the impoverished. Sit with them, talk with them, hear their stories, and simply be present for at least half an hour.

Later, take a half hour for yourself in some quiet place and contemplate the following questions:

- What part of myself do I see reflected in the eyes of these people?
- What part of them—and myself—do I reject?
- What part of myself do I prefer to give to?
- What part of myself do I refuse to give to?
- How can I go the step further to serve my fellow man without thought of rewarding or denying parts of myself?

Your New Way of Thinking

"I give from a place of right action. I accept the negative parts of myself as well as the positive parts. I give back in positive, loving ways because I am positive and loving to myself. I gain by not gaining for myself. I am selfless and in being so, find my true self."

Your Action Plan

Inner steps to take:

1. Take a piece of paper and make two vertical columns. Title the first column "Organizations/Causes I Like Giving To." Title the second column "Why I Give." List as many organizations and causes as you can, then the parallel reasons you want to give to them. For example, you might list a home

for pregnant teens and the reason you give there is because you once had a friend who had a child at fifteen. This will help you identify which needs you are fulfilling by giving.

2. Now take a second piece of paper and make two vertical columns. Title the first column "Organizations/Causes I Don't Like Giving To" and the second column "Why I Don't Give." List as many organizations and causes that you avoid giving to as you can, then the parallel reasons why you won't give or volunteer there. For example, you might list the state prison system, and the reason why you won't volunteer there is that you loathe criminals and believe they have no right to receive help. This will also help you identify which needs/fears you are fulfilling/denying by not giving.

3. Pick an unsavory (to you) but worthy organization or cause. Then, write out a small check and mail it to the organization or cause. First, however, before you mail it, hold the envelope with the check and focus your mind on it. Say to yourself, "This is an act of selfless giving. I have compassion for myself, therefore I have compassion for you." Then mail the check. The next day, write a paragraph about what it felt like to give at a new, more compassionate level.

4. Do a money or resource flowchart for yourself and/or your family (include volunteer work). Circle the areas in yellow where others benefit from your resource flow. Circle the areas in red where you benefit from your resource flow. (These may overlap.) Notice the colors in your "rainbow of giving." Remember, you can give money, labor, companionship, or love.

5. Consider what percentage of your time you give per year toward volunteer or giving work. If it's less than 5 to 10 percent, consider upping your giving time and resources.

6. Be charitable in ways that enable people's dignity. Don't just give a handout. Teach a skill, give someone an opportunity, or make a referral to help people help themselves.

7. Develop a spirit of gratitude, which will then often translate into giving. Gratitude, as someone once said, can turn "a

meal into a feast, a house into a home, a stranger into a friend."

8. Encourage young people in the act of giving. Read *Growing into Giving: Young People's Engagement with Charity* by Catherine Walker and Andrew Fisher, published by the British organization Charities Aid Foundation (*www.CAFonline.org/research*).

Financial steps to take:

1. Clear up your debt and reconstruct the flow from creditors to those in need.

2. Switch to a socially responsible credit card, like Co-Op America, or to affinity cards like those of the National Wildlife Federation or Sierra Club, for which a percentage of profits goes back to the organization.

3. Read *Investing from the Heart: The Guide to Socially Responsible Investments and Money Management* by Jack A. Brill and Alan Reder to learn about socially responsible business practices.

4. Read the Council of Economic Priorities's booklets on companies that are being socially responsible in the way they create and distribute their products and services. Align your investment strategies with like-minded organizations.

5. Make volunteering a family habit.

6. Consult the Charity Navigator at *www.charitynavigator.org* as a guide to intelligent giving. Know that small acts of charity can be as potent and as healing as large ones. Charity resonates, reminding us of what it means to be part of humankind.

7. Find a new money mantra. Say, "I give without thought of gain, but in order to find myself."

8. Give some money anonymously. In fact, give something every day to condition yourself to the habit of giving. Experience giving your money without being known for it or for expecting something in return. Give because of the desire to feel fully alive. Give from love, not from guilt.

9. Consider making gifts in the form of an endowment fund.

Think about It

"You give but little when you give of your possessions.
It is when you give of yourself that you truly give."
—Kahlil Gibran

THE GIVING GAME	
Rules	I give to maintain the flow of resources both to myself and to others.
Belief	I believe giving is the right thing to do, and sometimes I have both selfless and selfish motives.
Secret	I may not understand or be conscious of selfish motives for giving, but this is part of my human duality. Understanding how to give authentically is a process starting with my best intent.
Feeling	Self-satisfied, loving of others and self
Game Triggers	Abundance, fear, guilt, shame, altruism
Disarming Strategies	Understand your giving motives and give with the clearest intent possible.
Persona	Philanthropist or Philanthropist-Martyr
Action	Give at all levels and regularly with clear intent.

Giving Assessment

After the following statements, write *T* for those that are true for you, and *F* for those that are false.

1. I volunteer at least fifty hours per year. _____
2. I give some portion of my income as a tithe to organizations or worthwhile causes each year. _____
3. I usually discuss it with my partner before giving. _____
4. I give with discrimination. _____
5. I give without strings attached. _____
6. I don't give with a tax writeoff in mind as my primary motive. _____
7. My parents and loved ones taught me the value of giving while growing up. _____
8. I coach my family and loved ones about the value of giving.
   _____

9. I give anonymously sometimes. ____
10. I give because it makes me feel good inside. ____
11. I try to recycle clothes, furniture, and other resources that others might use them. ____
12. When I get a windfall or bonus, I generally give some portion of it away. ____

If you answered more than four of these as true, you are probably participating actively in a program of giving.

Chapter Seventeen

Game #15: The Simplify Game

Jeffrey's Story

Jeffrey was a successful CPA who had been in practice for twenty-five years. He passed his CPA exam almost right out of college and went to work with one of the major accounting firms. He worked there for ten years, then started his own practice doing corporate tax returns. Jeffrey had devoted much of his spare time, however, to his first love, pottery. He had spent years perfecting his skills as an artist. He had taken many classes in pottery and art, venturing as far as Santa Fe, Boston, and even England.

One day when Jeffrey was in his late forties, he had a wakeup call. His father died suddenly from cancer. The doctors had opened up Jeffrey's father to remove what they though might be a benign tumor in the intestinal cavity. They soon realized that a malignant, fast-growing cancer had spread throughout his body. He died shortly after.

Jeffrey was devastated. His father was only sixty-seven. After several months of contemplation, Jeffrey made a decision. He decided he had to pursue his purpose and passion in life before he, too, perished like his dad. He sold his accounting practice for

$200,000 cash and, at fifty, Jeffrey left the familiar world of accounting to pursue pottery. He liquidated some of his big-ticket assets, like his thirty-foot boat and summer home in Hawaii. He insisted his wife give up all but two of her credit cards. He turned in his three leased vehicles, and bought two reasonably priced, midsize cars. He stopped subsidizing his two daughters (now in their late teens) with $10,000-limit credit cards, and he cut down his golf club memberships to one. With his prudent savings—not touching his home value or retirement plan—he opened a small business to market his pottery. And he began a consistent program of tithing 10 percent of his annual income to local charities and organizations.

Jeffrey initially felt happy, but isolated. His accounting cohorts couldn't believe he had abandoned accounting for art. The majority of his friends thought he was crazy for leaving a thriving practice "when you are at the peak of your earning power." Very quickly, Jeffrey began to notice that his friends and associates started to withdraw. One of them told him privately that he felt threatened by Jeffrey's change of careers and simplified lifestyle. Soon, several colleagues stopped calling him. Jeffrey tried to make sense of this, and he soon realized that his values had changed. He had chosen to simplify, to do what he loved. He had decided to stop worshipping at the altar of money success, and had turned inward to find a balance between getting and giving back.

While he was happy, Jeffrey realized he had to face some facts. He had changed, but some of his friends hadn't. Some shunned him, and one finally admitted it was "too painful to see you making sacrifices, when I don't have the courage to do it." Other friends stayed in touch, but always tried to pick up the check for lunch or would talk down to him like he was a little child because he was "out of the financial biz." Some even tried to rescue him from a life they perceived was depressing and unhappy.

Jeffrey even heard through the grapevine how others pitied him for his present inability to live an upper-middle-class lifestyle. Jeffrey admitted that this much was true. He had chosen to simplify his life so he could live accountably with his money. He ultimately even sold his motorcycle and stopped taking expensive trips to exotic places. Jeffrey continued doing daily yoga, reading spiritual material every morning at 5:30 for one hour, and taking walks on the beach each day. Jeffrey volunteered to coach his nephew's soccer team, and he began teaching pottery at the local adult school. He was happy with his decision and knew he didn't want to lie on his deathbed wondering what life would have been like if he hadn't pursued his passion.

For the first three years, Jeffrey did experience symptoms of withdrawal from materialism. He would find himself feeling sorry that he couldn't participate in the critical games that he and his rich friends used to play when they would look down on those who just didn't have enough money to enjoy themselves well. But what kept Jeffrey inspired was the fire behind his vision of being the best potter he could become.

Unleashing his passion to create, and letting it flow bound-lessly, pushed Jeffrey through those hard times. He felt as if he had a beautiful gift to share with the world. He made a commitment to dedicate his next ten years to his vision and see where it took him. Jeffrey knew in his mind there would be no turning back. "Once I started following my soul's work," he said, "I knew I was committed for life and that accounting, at best, would only be a backup for what I do now." $

The Simplify Game: Living Light

Jeffrey courageously took up the Simplify Game. This is a game of paring down rather than gearing up. It's a game of conscious money use. It's a game of weighing our needs versus our wants, then making intelligent choices. It's essentially a game of "living light."

When we play this game, we've been motivated for some reason to live a conscious money lifestyle. If we decide to "live light," we begin to lighten up. We free ourselves of some of our financial baggage. Among others, Joe Dominguez and Vicki Robin (*Your Money or Your Life*) made famous the concept of achieving financial independence through living a simplified money experience.

For Dominguez and Robin, a simplified existence means transforming our relationship with money. It means that making money takes a backseat to real living. It means setting up life priorities so that we can focus on what's fulfilling for us, rather than on getting what the other guy has. Simplifying means working smart with what money we do have. It means being focused on what we need, but little more.

Typically in our culture, when we start to get a little money, we start acquiring things. Then these things take caring for. We become defined and driven by the maintenance of these objects, and soon we have lots of stuff and lots of debt or, at least, lots of obligations. We start to get owned by our stuff, and pretty soon we are working very hard for it. Dominguez calls this "making a dying" rather than making a living.

The Simplify Game is based on financial independence. That means having enough money to cover real and perceived needs, wants, and desires, plus having enough money coming in so we don't have to do anything for money. It's based on using money as an asset; having little or no debt; focusing on healthy relationships with others, our money, and ourselves. It also means being responsible to do what we love. It means taking a responsible stance by giving back to the community. It means planning thoughtfully for the future.

The Belief

Whether we are rich, poor, or somewhere in between, we can play the Simplify Game. All it takes is a will to jettison the baggage of the other Money Games and the surfeit of stuff in our lives, and get down to basics.

It's really a game based on sufficiency, with the idea being that if you let go of what you're trying to get more of, this frees up energy to do the best with what you already have. Those who live by the Simplify Game, live simply.

We buy what we need, no more. We stop shopping for sport. We keep an older car despite imperatives to buy the latest SUV. We live with one or two televisions, not three or four. We pare down, recycle, use things over, stretch leftovers, watch for sales, cut back on nonnecessities, and put our energy into what we need.

We also learn to do a few of the things we used to pay others to do for us. This could be simple car maintenance, modest home repair, our own taxes, basic clothing repairs, washing out sweaters instead of paying for dry cleaning, occasionally taking a bag lunch instead of always eating out. It means minimizing our spending. It means really asking ourselves, "Do I need this? Or do I just want this? Am I buying it because someone else has it?"

The Secret

The secret of the Simplify Game is the willingness to give up greed. Greed is the fear that there is never enough, and so we must have more than we actually need. We are basically a greed-based society. Greed has become the emotional energy that fuels our outward display of opulence. We've been acculturated to demonstrate our value to the outside world by how much wealth we can display. So we think *more, more, more* will show we are successful, wise, and powerful.

To play the Simplify Game means we must jettison many of our society's values. It means rebuilding our values around an internal, rather than an external, concept of worth. In individual psychology terms, it means unhooking from outdated parental (societal) values and thinking for ourselves. It means deciding what *we* need rather than handing over that task to whomever decides such things at NBC, General Motors, or the *New York Times*. It means growing up, taking charge of our adult lives, and gaining independence. While we may choose to have some of the things touted by Madison Avenue, we'll do so as a conscious choice and based on our values.

Game Triggers

Fortunately or unfortunately, triggers for the Simplify Game often surface when we experience a galvanizing event that wakes us up to consciousness. In that wrenching moment, we are forced to examine our core values. We sit up. We take notice. We look around and ask ourselves, *"Is this the legacy I want to leave?"* We begin to ask ourselves, *"When is it enough?"* We begin to face the reality that our stuff will never make us whole, will never stop the march of living and dying, will never justify who we've been and how we've lived.

Triggers can include:

- A life-threatening or near-death experience
- Going bankrupt
- Losing a parent to illness, disease, or accident
- Having an epiphany or other moment of unusually clear realization. This sometimes occurs during or after a major accident; a brush with fire, flood, or earthquake; or a child's near death.
- Losing retirement savings in a bear market
- Having business or resources stolen or confiscated
- Having a close friend or colleague get arrested for fraud or other money-related crime
- Becoming critically ill
- Beginning to explore family life or money history through groups, seminars, or individual counseling
- Experiencing a divorce or spouse's death

Disarming Strategies

If you decide to play this game, start with detachment. You will want to detach yourself from your debilitating beliefs about money. This means eliminating the constant energy you divert to thoughts about money based on fear, including fear spawned by the community you live in and those with whom you work and socialize. It also will mean detaching from the national bias toward wealth and power.

If you abandon the countless hours spent contemplating what life would be like with more money, you clear a path toward new possibilities. You let go of fear and embrace trust. You find ways to be independent with your money. You seek ways to gain freedom from organizations and jobs that control you. You allow yourself a chance to return to a relationship where you are connected to a life vision that has meaning for you, not merely to a career that produces income.

Simplification usually means fewer bills. Because your vocation is your life passion, there no longer is any such thing as "work." What used to be work is now your joy. You no longer find yourself needing to escape from a tough day at the office and spend more money to escape from the pain you're in. You won't revert to shopping trips, expensive meals, or exorbitant health clubs to relieve the stress. You won't participate in negative addictions to ease your suffering.

Your biggest challenge will be to differentiate weekend days from weekdays because you will be doing what brings you pleasure all the time. You may have deadlines when tasks need to be completed, but you won't mind doing them because you will be discovering a creative side of yourself that loves to live playfully. You will be motivated to maintain a balanced life shared among family/friends, your passion, and your self-actualization.

Be ready for some significant changes in your life, however. During simplification you may radically change your thoughts about yourself and how you see money. Changing repetitive, unhealthy money thoughts will cause a shift in how you operate in the world. When you change how you see yourself at the workplace, in the home, and with friends, you'll also change how you project yourself out into the world. Be prepared for some friendships to end. Be ready for other people to not understand why you are simplifying. Your new focus will force them to put a mirror up to their own lives. This could be threatening. Abandoning a money-cures-all belief system sometimes is too much for people conditioned to living a life immersed in Money Games. How they operate with their own money could come into question. And your reflection will be the cause.

As you simplify, you will keep some old associates, but you will also develop new friends with similar, soulful ways of thinking. But this may take time. First, you must face the mirror and look at where you have come from, then decide where you are headed.

When change is invited in we have a choice: Embrace it, shift into denial, or dismiss it. If you embrace it, you will most likely witness the death of the old ways with money. You may even mourn the loss of those old ways of being. This period of adjustment might feel uncomfortable and unproductive, but it is needed to clear out the old Money Games you used to play. You may feel a period of disorientation, even malaise, while your old ways of thinking give way to new, more balanced thoughts.

You may experience discomfort before your new path can be completely revealed.

Usually this passes after a few months. As you connect to new money thinking, your future will come into focus. Your intent for a simplified life will take shape as concrete actions and decisions. Now you will be less affected by the old money thoughts and better able to catch yourself from getting hooked into old Money Game patterns. You'll be able to control your money emotions, stop participating in money dramas, and channel more energy and time into living your life in a focused, essential way.

Simplification can have many aims. It can seek merely to lower the money stress in your life so you cut back on expenses by selling your home and renting a studio apartment. Others choose to downsize or simplify so that they can pursue their life mission. Whatever your initial intent, you must first define your motive. If you aren't clear regarding your basic intention to simplify, it may backfire on you as you may become resentful about why you had to give up some of your material possessions. Try writing out a paragraph or two on the following:

- Why am I simplifying?
- Make a list of the qualities you admire about someone who has simplified and what attracts you about their lifestyle.
- What will I miss from my old life?
- What planning steps will I take to begin a simplifying process?
- Can I get by with less than what greed has led me to believe?

Consider what small steps you can take toward the simplification process right now. List ten things you and your family could do right now to simplify, such as eating out only once a week, taking bag lunches, cutting back on shopping trips, and carpooling.

Your New Way of Thinking

"I disengage from self-sabotaging money beliefs, and simplify my life and my actions with money. I live in the moment, knowing I have enough. I have made myself independent of people, places, and things. I am at peace."

Your Action Plan

Inner steps to take:

1. Read *Your Money or Your Life* by Joe Dominguez and Vicki Robin.
2. Put together a simplification plan. If you leap into this game without planning, you may end up feeling dissatisfied. So take into account the following:
   - What areas can you simplify most easily?
   - What areas will take three to six months to simplify?
   - What new investment or money strategies will you want to explore?
   - If you are going to make a career change, consider how long this will take you and what steps you will have to

take to take this new direction (education, cutting back on current job, relocating, etc.).

- Analyze whether you have enough capital to carry you for the first two years as you try this new vocation you are passionate about.
- If you are part of a couple, make sure you are both on the same page about simplification.

3. Begin to simplify by:
- Living within your means. That requires waiting until you have the money before you buy something.
- Curbing the need to impress people . . . including Mom or Dad.
- Not seeking other people's approval; seek just your own.
- Deferring shopping except when you intend to buy. Control the desire to window-shop as a pastime—it fuels your desire like smelling a plate of brownies or a cup of coffee.
- Turning off television shows like the Home Shopping Network. They use addictive principles to convince you to buy. Get smart and give up the habit.

4. Volunteer and see how people and organizations function with less.

5. Manage your health. Eat healthily, get adequate rest, and give up habits like smoking or excessive alcohol consumption that later can cost you thousands in hospital bills and medication.

Financial steps to take:

1. Consult with a fee-only planner to help you seek financial independence through investments or new money strategies.

2. Cut up your credit cards. Face the reality that if you get enslaved by credit-card debt, you have no more autonomy than you did when you used to ask Mom or Dad for your allowance. Cut the cord with credit-card companies.

3. Research your purchases. Read consumer reports and make intelligent buys.

4. When you must shop, shop smart. Watch for discounts, wait for off-season sales, and shop at consolidators or clubs that specialize in making large buys and then passing the savings onto you.
5. Consider buying things used.
6. Commit yourself to paying off your mortgage as soon as possible.
7. Save money every single month.
8. Gang up your errands to save gas and time.
9. Try public transportation, at least occasionally.
10. Co-op with neighbors to share big-ticket purchases, like snowblowers, lawn mowers, and leaf blowers.
11. Make a hobby out of a service or volunteering.

Think about It

"Money may be only a means to another end. So the challenge rests in earning money to live life, rather than living to earn money."

—Michael Toms

THE SIMPLIFY GAME	
Rules	I evolve to a simplified life, where I have financial and personal independence.
Belief	I understand my money beliefs and take appropriate responsible action with money in my life. I simplify and follow my passion.
Secret	I may give up a few things and lose a few friends along the way, but I will focus my passion and my money.
Feeling	Relief, freedom
Game Triggers	Galvanizing life events or self-knowledge
Disarming Strategies	I make the commitment to simplifying, then plan for my independence.
Persona	Conscientious Money Practitioner
Action	Simplify, focus, and take passionate action.

Simplify Your Life Plan

Here are some suggested steps to follow in developing your simplification plan:

1. Make a list of what really makes you happy in your life.
2. Make a list of your most valued possessions. Consider giving away one or two of them.
3. Develop a vision and mission statement for your life. Figure out how much money it will take to live this life.
4. Determine your net worth (assets minus liabilities).
5. Make sure there is synergy between your life work and your vision and mission statement regarding how you want to live your life.
6. Write down why you are simplifying and make sure it resonates with your life's purpose so you won't become resentful later.
7. Set up a one-, three-, five-, ten-, and twenty-year plan for how your life will look and when you expect your simplifying plan to be complete.
8. Do the small things first. Pay off credit cards, consider paying off your mortgage (if you plan on keeping your house). Try living on your reduced budget for a while before you actually change your job or location to see if you can be disciplined enough.
9. Run your plan by a financial counselor and have a therapist review your vision and mission statement.
10. Keep a journal to monitor feelings and thoughts with money that might be part of your withdrawal process as you simplify.
11. Become aware of your money thoughts by checking your motives behind purchases, and at the end of the month, review what you have bought or refrained from buying.
12. If you have a partner, make sure you are both on the same page and want to simplify and have common goals with how your money will be used to support your future.

Chapter Eighteen

Playing Healthy Money Games

Tim and Candice's Story

Tim and Candice live a good life, though it's well below their means. While still enjoying the finer material things, they keep their spending and liabilities in balance with their income and assets. They drive new cars like a Chevy Suburban or a Volkswagen, but not flashy, enormously expensive cars like a BMW or a Mercedes. They live in a nice, middle- to upper-middle-class area, but not in the wealthiest part of town. Their children go to private Catholic schools, but not the expensive, upper-crust schools nearby. They work through their problems in life and don't put on appearances about having everything perfect.

Tim and Candice both "come from money," but you wouldn't know this. Educated at good colleges, they are well read. Neither of them has had to work, but both have maintained full-time, middle-income jobs. They both have found time to volunteer and serve on community boards in addition to being parents of three children. They both believe in healthy exercise that they make time for each day. Neither has taken advantage of plastic surgery or other such appearance enhancement; both look their forty-five years.

Over many years working as the couple's financial advisor, I discovered that the pair had a considerable amount of money. Not your typical "trust fund babies," both Tim and Candice have donated money and time to friends and charities in need. They have done their best to teach their children appropriate morals and ethics, and have modeled a right-living lifestyle. They take regular but fairly modest vacations, spending time with their children. "If someone asked us," they state, "we would say we do indeed have money, but we try to live on our salaries, invest wisely, and live a harmonious life. We don't deprive ourselves, but we don't overinflate what we have or what we are, either." $

Healthy Games: Keeping Your Balance

The key to evolving healthy Money Games is balance. That is, when we both give and receive in responsible ways, our negative games pass away. They get replaced by a collection of positive money behaviors that help us and others.

Like any skill, healthy money practices can be learned. As this book has shown, most of us learned Money Games from generations before us or from the financial gurus and culture of the day. We have very little opportunity to learn, understand, and practice healthy money skills. But this remains an option, and many are demonstrating a wonderful sense of freedom and compassion with money when they use healthy money practices.

Healthy Money Games begin with a centered, balanced game plan. We start with a clear understanding of who we are, what our money triggers are, and how we get our needs met in a variety of ways, including money. Then we learn how we can be comfortable with money as a portion of our world, but not as the dominant theme.

With self-knowledge, we can then begin to understand how our money beliefs play out in our outer world in relationships, careers, and lifestyle. Armed with knowledge of our "outer money self," we can make more balanced choices about what we want and don't want in our world. When we "out" our money secrets, both in our internal world and in our outer world, the closet gets cleared out. We give up the hidden agendas and manipulations. When these go, the stress, anxiety, and money tension go with them. We can find a center of peace with money that manifests in healthy choices, solid decisions, and wise money actions.

The secret behind healthy Money Games is that we've been courageous enough to uncover and release our old money secrets. The secrets simply dry up and blow away. Like old nightmares that wrench us awake, money secrets that we expose to the light of understanding and compassion wither and die. They are no longer secrets because we have owned them. They no longer hold us in a death grip because we finally know who we are with money. We will never have to hide anything again because we already know we can cope with the worst of our money fears.

The secret is that there are no secrets. We are open. We give up manipulating. We stop being codependent on money and stand in equal power with money. We don't participate in relationships that are based solely on money unless we consciously choose to. We don't sacrifice ourselves for money or money deals. We feel good about money actions and therefore we feel good about our money actions with others. We put money in service to ourselves instead of being in service to it.

When we place money in an appropriate place, we find the rest of life emerges. We find that the money veil lifts to reveal a freer world inside and outside ourselves, filled with people, contribution, social awareness, and conscious action. We use money as it was intended to be used: to better ourselves, our community, and our world in wise, centered ways.

Specifically, what does this mean? It means we make mature decisions with money. We balance our hierarchy of needs, so that no one need bloats our existence. We don't deny ourselves, but we also don't deny our social responsibility. We give to ourselves and our loved ones as much as to others, but we do it out of compassion, not out of fear. We operate in trust, not greed. We think about giving before we think about getting. We think circulation, not hoarding. We connect with the network of humanity, rather than wall ourselves in a tower of money terror.

Some New Games to Try

The following are some of the healthy Money Games that come into play once we get clearly focused on who we are, what we want, and how we want to do it.

The Financial Literacy Game

Once we realize we have a right and responsibility to know about money, we give up our position of ignorance. We start the Financial Literacy Game by educating ourselves. We can attend a class, pick up a book, get financial coaching, or join a financial or investment group. We don't have to be financial wizards, but we want to at least get a knowledge of money basics. Any of these approaches steers us onto the road to playing a savvy financial game that puts us in control of our minds and our money.

Financial literacy also includes a basic determination of our true bottom line. This means coming to terms with what we owe and deducting these liabilities from our assets to derive a net worth. There are no emotions attached to this outcome. This final number is our financial reality, pure and simple. Financial literacy is knowing this bottom-line number, then being responsible, accountable, and honest with others and ourselves regarding our money. It is understanding how to make our assets and money work for us, rather than feeling victimized by forces outside our control from ignorance or lack of agency. Financial literacy means we open our eyes to our true financial position.

We can then up our financial IQ simply by taking charge of learning how to make our money work for us. Just this act of upping our financial IQ—gaining understanding and learning how to manage our resources—will eliminate a third of the Money Games in this book.

The Wise Money Game

Money wisdom comes with learning, understanding, and experience. This game is played when we use self-knowledge, financial knowledge, and responsible action to live money-wise in the world. The first place to start playing the Wise Money Game is to explore our money history, our money heritage, and our current money story. That is, we need to take an honest look at how we are operating with money. We can then stop hiding our own motives from ourselves. We can start making informed money choices.

When we delve into our personal drivers, biases, and beliefs about money, we gain enormous power. We begin to understand the meaning of money in our lives. We can then divest ourselves of belief systems that lock us into lives of fear, anger, greed, and scarcity. We can then adopt beliefs that serve us better. We can form solid money beliefs and values that give each of us a sense of peace and rightness, not heartburn.

When we arrive at this place, we know it. We know it in our heads, our hearts, and our gut. We breathe easy. We relax. We sleep well. We gain a deep sense of rightness about how to live. Above all, we are at peace. Each of us knows when we hit that "sweet spot."

When we can couple that abiding peace with our newfound money knowledge, we then become the master of money in our lives. We manage how we live in the world with money and see (and forgive) our own contradictions. We are able to enjoy our innate humanness, perhaps laughing at the actions we take because we are, after all, human beings evolving, not having arrived.

As Money Masters, we turn toward the truth of ourselves, not away. We put money in its place, as a channel for our unique expressions. We stop framing money as evil. We see it as a blessing, a resource. We view it for the ultimate purpose, authentic caring.

The Healthy Money Relationship Game

When we are ready, we'll shine the light in our emotional money closets. That is, we will own up to our stuff, our games, our self-serving dependencies, our ugly money deals, as well as the compassionate ways we also help ourselves, our families, and others. The more we own up, the more real we become to ourselves. We discover that we've done the best we could with the tools we had. And we will finally forgive ourselves; we will release and move on. We will then be able emotionally to forgive others.

We find relief when we can stop blaming, pointing fingers, dragging the past around everywhere we go, and making the same money mistakes over and over. We can finally give up the pain. One of the first steps in evolving a healthy money relationship is to get in touch with our money pain, which is typically a symptom of anger about money. It will be one of the first, strongest emotions we have when we start exploring our emotional life with money. Once we hit our anger goldmine, we can work through it. It's rich in passion. We'll then probably experience some grief, some loss for what "might have been" or "what we really deserved." The reality is we are right where we are, digesting this book, seeking a new way.

Once we hit that anger, that grief, and that loss, we have to begin to release it. We can write the feelings down on a piece or paper, and then burn it. Or we can write a daily journal about it, then tear it up. Or tell someone about our losses, our hurts, our anguish. The point is to get it out and tell it to keep on moving. We will then have taken charge of our emotions.

One of the secrets about money emotions is that, as in all areas of human life, we feel and think things that are meant to exist in the moment. They are meant to come, and then to go. The *going* is the key part. They are meant to be felt and experienced, but not to hang around as if in concrete. So take heart in knowing that each of us can cope with our own selves, and that if we had the emotions, we can also cope with owning them and then releasing them.

This gives us great power to confront our money feelings. Once confronted, we can then take that great power and passion and move it out into the world as we relate to life and money in a conscious-self mode. We will not be able to be manipulated anymore. We will know ourselves. We will know our triggers and be able to deal with them. We won't engage in one-up, one-down relationships with people, institutions, or the world because we will find our voice to speak up for ourselves. We will know we have the right to live in freedom with ourselves and our money.

We can actually then evolve a new money story—a story for now. Because the fact is that we live in the now, not yesterday. We have charge of today; no one else does. Like clicking on the "refresh" button on our computer screen, we can refresh our money lives. We can create our own money self, standing anew with our self-evolved money thoughts and beliefs—and no one else's. We than can go through all the steps in evolving a real relationship with our money.

Millie's Story

Millie used to work for a natural-gas company. She rented the same modest ocean-view apartment for more than twenty years. She was intelligent, a hard worker who made a middle-class salary. Millie was an independent thinker who stood up for women's causes and others as well. She was the first woman to run different divisions in her company as well as to hold jobs that only men before her had held.

Millie enjoyed life, traveled widely, but she also saved for the future. She took foreign trips annually, trekking from Africa to Asia. She gave freely to causes and embraced the view that by helping others, her generosity would come back to her as well.

When I met Millie on one of these foreign trips, she was sixty. She had saved well, been prudent with her money, yet continued her program of active giving. She had been able to retire at age fifty. Caring for her fellow man had always been an important value for her, and she demonstrated this again during the trip. When I accompanied Millie on this Third World exploration, by the end of the trip she had given away the majority of her clothes, money, and food to the people we visited. When others questioned this, Millie said, "I've got plenty to keep me going and enjoy my life. Why not share it?"

Interestingly, when Millie turned sixty-two, she told me she had suddenly inherited several hundred thousand dollars. However, she was determined to go right on living the same way. Her only new purchase was a small cabin on ten acres in the middle of nowhere. "Like always, I do some things for myself, some things for others. I feel at peace with myself." I saw Millie last year on a flight to China. Nearing seventy, she looked as chipper as ever. She was still traveling to foreign countries. "Just been to Bali to show my commitment to foreign travel despite the terrorist bombings there. No sense in giving over to nonsense," she laughed. $

The Healthy Parent Money Game

Once we've evolved our money wisdom and knowledge, we can turn to coaching our children in how to evolve a healthy relationship with money.

Our children will watch what we do with our money. They will watch what areas of life we convert to a money question. They will notice what we solve with money, or fail to solve. They will scrutinize how we balance with money the tangible and intangible, our inner and outer worlds. They will learn both our good and our bad habits. So we have a choice: Do we pass on our ignorance or our wisdom?

Educating our children about money starts with teaching them the facts of money life. Great resources to explore are the books of Robert Kiyosaki, who wrote *Rich Dad, Poor Dad*. In an entertaining, clear way, he teaches basic financial skills from the perspective of a young boy seeking an understanding of money issues from his two dads, one money savvy, the other education savvy. With this book and others, adults can learn how to coach children and teens to take charge of their money starting at a very young age. Some skills to teach include:

- Getting and keeping a job
- Making money
- Understanding assets versus liabilities
- Evolving healthy money habits
- Working with others to manage, make, and share money
- Monitoring our priorities with money
- Evolving toward financial independence

Our children absorb much more through our money actions than we are aware. Confusion for our children arises when our acts with money don't match our words, such as, for example, when we say we don't have enough money to buy them a skateboard and then purchase a new car. This leaves kids in a state of incongruence, especially if there isn't any dialogue with the parents. This is how Money Games begin to form for our offspring.

Appropriate money parenting will teach our children how to be open and independent with money. We will be able to help them avoid our old money mythologies that may have been handed down to us out of well-intentioned but misguided ignorance. We will coach them early on how to be Money Masters instead of money slaves.

The Social Responsibility Game

The Social Responsibility Game gives us an outlet to share our new money persona and practices. Playing this game, we use our money to best serve ourselves and others in enlightened ways.

We can use money as a power source. We can use it to open up opportunities, to heal, to build bridges. Assuming social responsibility with money is one of the most valuable healthy games we can play both at an individual and an organizational level.

Individual responsibility

On an individual level, we can use our resources to take responsible money action. That is, we can become conscious of the fact that personal money decisions we make ripple out into our community and beyond. When we opt for buying Styrofoam cups instead of reusing a travel cup over and over, we are contributing in a small way to pollution and waste. When we choose to buy a SUV, we are making the choice to use up lots of gasoline, which ultimately impacts world markets and global warming. I am not saying we should stop any of these things. I am saying we need to make *conscious* choices.

On the other hand, when we decline to help fund shelters for abandoned children and hope someone else will pick up the slack, we are putting blinders on to being part of a community. When we invest in polluting corporations rather than environmentally conscious ones, we may be making money in the short term, but we are also contributing to the destruction of our environment in the long run. Native Americans believe people need to be socially conscious enough to consider how their decisions will impact the next seven generations. If we are not similarly making choices in the context of what it will mean for our children and their children and their children's children, then we are living in a myopic bubble of self-interest.

We need to use our individual money to support our beliefs and values. Whenever we make a purchase or give money we are voting with our dollars. This means we are throwing our support toward those who profit from our exchanges of energy.

For instance, shopping at a store that was just proven to have supported sexual discrimination means we indirectly support sexual discrimination, especially if the organization pays a fine without making fundamental changes to ensure this doesn't happen again. When we endorse the organization's behavior by buying, we are, in fact, turning our backs on what is appropriate for all humans.

Improving human consciousness with money can even be taken a step further. When we give money to a charity, do we really know how much reaches the people or causes for which it was intended? The more aware we are of how we use money and where it goes, the better the chance of our bringing health to the world with money. Each simple money act we make with awareness unites us together in a common positive action toward wholeness and goodwill.

Corporate responsibility

In the best of all worlds, the organizations and corporations to which we belong and have interest in will extend the Healthy Money Game ethic to conscious money actions both here and abroad. This will mean a commitment to:

- Using natural resources wisely
- Capitalizing on human resources in a profit-sharing, possibly open-book format (in which accounting practices and

profit-and-loss dynamics are revealed to all) and treating employees with financial respect

- Committing to giving back a portion of gross assets to socially responsible causes
- Creating goods and services with an eye toward ethical responsibility to the community as a whole
- Modeling appropriate leadership behaviors with money
- Treating other companies as partners rather than enemies
- Conducting business with an eye to the next generation and those who follow

A good model for socially responsible corporate practices is the platform of the Coalition for Environmentally Responsible Economies (CERES). Formed in 1989, the Boston-based organization encourages businesses to become more attentive to the environment.

Other resources for responsible organizational action include KLD Research & Analytics, Inc., which promotes global socially responsible investing by providing corporate social research products and services to institutional investors; SocialFunds.com, which features over 10,000 pages of information on socially responsible mutual funds, community investments, corporate research, shareowner actions, and daily social investment news; and David A. Schwerin's *Conscious Capitalism: Principles for Prosperity,* which integrates business practices with ageless wisdom principles.

Sharon and Dan's Story

Sharon and Dan had recently inherited from Sharon's parents $500,000 after taxes. The money came in the form of a well-balanced portfolio of stocks, bonds, and mutual funds.

Sharon was a teacher, and Dan was an engineer. Until this point, Sharon had let Dan manage all of their money. However, with this large sum of newfound wealth dropping into their laps, Sharon was determined to manage it herself. Within a couple of years, all of Sharon and Dan's children were in college or working on their own. Sharon felt it was now her responsibility to do the right thing with the remaining money.

She started taking some investment classes at a university, and then took a class on ethics and morals. Prior to becoming wealthy, Sharon had always invested what small amount of money she had of her own in socially conscious mutual funds. Sharon now began to wonder about the companies in which her money was invested. Were those companies doing good things for the world? She struggled whether to sell shares of companies that weren't.

Sharon started ordering annual reports for all of the new portfolio stocks as well as for those in her previous portfolio with Dan. She wasn't sure what to look for exactly, but began researching how, where, and why they did their business and whether they were operating responsibly in the world.

After her research, Sharon made a decision. She became convinced that because she had this large sum of money, she needed to be completely responsible with it. She decided, therefore, to take $100,000 and set up a foundation to fund projects she thought would benefit the world. In addition to her funding efforts, she also gave $500 each month to a worthy charity. Sharon told her husband she had created a full-time job for herself based on being an accountable steward of this money. "I feel I am making the world a better place based on these actions. I feel good about having money, but even better about using it responsibly." $

Arming Strategies for Healthy Games

Naturally, the arming strategies for healthy games include self-exploration, study, a will toward right action, and a desire to act with authenticity around money issues.

In addition to others strategies detailed above, consider:

- Doing the work you love, even if it is as an avocation for a while. This will get your consciousness moving in the right direction and activate your passion.
- Eliminating dependency, addictions, and other bad habits. This will clear your head (and soul) for conscious action.
- Tune into an awareness of your own longevity. As Joe Dominguez says in *Your Money or Your Life*, "Someone who is 40 years old has 260,000 hours of life left on an actuarial table. How will we use the 260,000 hours? How will we spend it?"
- Find support in spirituality. Many books support positive causes, such as global peace or a clean environment. Open your heart to a cause that attracts you.

Your New Way of Thinking

"I play only healthy Money Games. I know myself and am known by the responsible actions I take with money."

Your Action Plan

1. Remove your wallet. Hold it in your hand for a moment. Take out the one thing that most represents you. What did you take out? Money? A photo? An identification or membership card of some kind? Look at it and then ask yourself, "Is this what I want to spend the rest of my life being, doing, having, sharing?"
2. Write your own money obituary in two paragraphs. Consider how you want to be remembered in your money practices.
3. Find other human beings to relate to on a search for truth and meaning, not just the search for money.
4. Understand your needs hierarchy completely.
5. Know when to let go. Know when to hold on. If we let go wisely, we quickly find ways in which to renew our wealth.
6. Consider other avenues to center your money practices, like

your local church, synagogue, temple, mosque, or spiritual gathering. If we learn what's going on in our economy and in our government, then perhaps we can help share our knowledge and solve our social problems.

7. Meet monthly for breakfast with a group of service-oriented individuals. Brainstorm and act as a sounding board to support each other's right actions with money.

Creating a Money Plan

Possessed of financial knowledge and a healthy relationship with money, you can turn your vision into reality with a strategic personal money plan. Consider starting with these steps:

Step One: Create a vision by visualizing what you want your life to look like in the future.

Step Two: Write out what your personal mission will be, based on your vision. Vision and mission statements usually have a purpose that is to benefit all humans, not just ourselves. Your personal mission will probably include phrases like:

- "My life in the future will include . . ."
- "My work situation will be . . ."
- "My day-to-day living style will be . . ."
- "My family will be . . ."
- "My colleagues will be people who . . ."
- "My money management will include . . ."
- "My passion will be expressed by . . ."

Step Three: Decide how much money you will need to carry out your vision and mission.

Step Four: Ask yourself if this is attainable and if you are willing to devote the energy it will require to realize this vision and mission.

Step Five: Complete a detailed timeline of how you will reach your goals over the next one, three, five, ten, and twenty years. The more specific you are, the better the chance of achieving your vision/mission.

Step Six: Take action. After you have a plan, run it by a financial expert to see if it has merit. If so, begin to make your vision a reality. Remember to stay in balance in all areas of your life while striving to live your vision.

Think about It

"In the quiet hours when we are alone and there is nobody to tell us what fine fellows we are, we come sometimes upon a moment in which we wonder not how much money we are earning, nor how famous we have become, but what good we are doing."

—A.A. Milne

HEALTHY MONEY GAMES	
Rules	Healthy money games have a centered, balanced game plan, developed around clear self-knowledge, needs, and desires appropriately expressed.
Belief	I am responsible with myself and my money.
Secret	There are no secrets.
Feeling	Balanced, at peace
Game Triggers	Ground-zero realization about myself
Arming Strategies	I get educated, face my fears, confront my money dysfunctions, and evolve a healthy set of money actions.
Persona	Money Master
Action	Own, feel, release, get conscious, take action.

Recommended Reading

Rabbi Milton Bonder, *The Kabbala of Money: Insights on Livelihood, Business and All Forms of Economic Behavior* (Shambhala, 1996).

Jack A. Brill and Alan Reder, *Investing From the Heart: The Guide to Socially Responsible Investments and Money Management* (Crown, 1992).

Richard Carlson, *Don't Worry, Make Money: Spiritual and Practical Ways to Create Abundance and More Fun in Your Life* (Little, Brown, 1998).

Joe Dominguez and Vicki Robin, *Your Money or Your Life: Transforming Your Relationship with Money and Achieving Financial Independence* (Viking Penguin, 1992).

Edgar Z. Friedenberg, *The Vanishing Adolescent* (Greenwood, 1985).

Adrian Furnham and Michael Argyle, *The Psychology of Money* (Routledge, 1998).

Ivan Illich, *Deschooling Society* (Marion Boyars Publishing, 1999).

Natalie H. Jenkins et al., *You Paid How Much for That?: How to Win at Money Without Losing at Love* (Jossey-Bass, 2002).

George Kinder, *Seven Stages of Money Maturity: Understanding the Spirit and Value of Money in Your Life* (Delacorte, 1999).

Robert Kiyosaki, *Rich Dad, Poor Dad: What the Rich Teach Their Kids About Money—That the Poor and Middle Class Do Not!* (Warner, 2000).

Olivia Mellan, *Money Harmony: Resolving Money Conflicts in Your Life and Your Relationships* (Walker, 1995).

Julie Morgenstern, *Organizing from the Inside Out: The Foolproof System for Organizing Your Home, Your Office, and Your Life* (Owl Books, 1998).

Jacob Needleman, *Money and the Meaning of Life* (Currency/Doubleday, 1994).

Jacob Needleman et al., *Money, Money, Money: The Search for Wealth and the Pursuit of Happiness* (Hay House, 1998).

Deborah L. Price, *Money Therapy: Using the Eight Money Types to Create Wealth and Prosperity* (New World Library, 2002).

David A. Schwerin, *Conscious Capitalism: Principles for Prosperity* (Butterworth-Heinemann, 1998).

Barbara Wilder, *Money Is Love: Reconnecting to the Sacred Origins of Money* (Wild Ox Press, 1999).

Index